Knowing God through the Liturgy

by
Peter Toon

FOR

Dan and Mickey
Edward and Martha
and all the ESA
folks at Nacogdoches

Knowing God Through The Liturgy

1992 © The Prayer Book Society Publishing Company

Published June 1992 by

The Prayer Book Society Publishing Company
A Division of the Prayer Book Society of the Episcopal Church
P. O. Box 268
Largo, Florida 34649-0268

ISBN 1-879793-01-6

CONTENTS

Preface

1. The American Experience   1

2. Liturgy since Cranmer   9

3. What knowing is   18

4. Covenant with God   27

5. Baptism and Confirmation   40

6. Morning and Evening Prayer   48

7. Praying the Psalter   62

8. Holy Communion   80

9. The Church Year   94

10. Common Prayer   103

11. Language for God   116

12. God is Love   133

PREFACE

It is a privilege to be invited by the Prayer Book Society to write a book to be published under its name. To be an Anglican is for me to be committed to that Common Prayer Tradition which began in England in 1549 and continued through a series of editions of *Books of Common Prayer* throughout the world until the 1960s.

My title recalls a booklet I wrote for Grove Booklets of Nottingham, England, in the early 1970s entitled, *Knowing God through the Liturgy*. I hope that over the last twenty years I have grown in knowledge and wisdom and that this much longer study is a vast improvement on the previous effort. My recent writing has been in the area of meditation and contemplation [see, e.g. my *Meditating as a Christian (1991); and Spiritual Companions: Introducing 100 Spiritual Classics (1992)*] but it has been a joy to switch to the theological reflection upon liturgy.

This book has been written during Lent in my fifteenth and sixteenth months as a resident alien in America. Its themes have engaged my mind at all times when I was not teaching in class or preaching in various parts of the country. I hope that though written fairly quickly it has within it the fruit of my thinking over two decades or so since my ordination as a priest of the Church of England.

I must thank my wife, Vita, for her careful reading of the text, and my daughter, Debbie, for her patience with an absent father. My learned colleague, the Revd Dr Charles Caldwell, has passed on his wisdom to me in frequent conversations, and John Jamieson, an enthusiast for the Common Prayer Tradition has helped me gain access to important sources. Crews Giles, a student at Nashotah House, has kindly assisted me with word processing and in technical matters while John and Diane Ott in Florida have given me their courteous and professional help in producing the book for publication by the Prayer Book Society. I must also mention the help and encouragement of Graham Eglington, the National Director of the Prayer Book Society of Canada, and his colleagues.

Of course I take responsibility for what is written and I place it in the hands of God to do with as is pleasing unto Him.

I have written it in such a way that it speaks both to the American Episcopal and Canadian Anglican Churches. I hope also that friends back in England will appreciate its contents. The book is dedicated to four East Texans and their friends who gave me gracious hospitality recently. May our Lord bless them abundantly.

Peter Toon
Nashotah House, Wisconsin
Holy Week, 1992.

1

THE AMERICAN EXPERIENCE

We arrived in this country on December 31, 1990, and, having missed our connection in New York at JFK for Milwaukee, had to spend New Year's Eve in the city before leaving very early on January 1, 1991 for Wisconsin, via St Louis. The culture shock of New York City on New Year's Eve has been as nothing compared with the culture shocks I've felt within the Episcopal Church, which is so different in many ways from the Church of England.

First shock

The first shock was to discover that many bishops actually forbade the use of the *BCP* (1928) and did so even at funerals of people who had used the Book for most if not all of their lives. My surprise and dismay were increased since it was from the mouths of bishops who I thought to be reasonably conservative that I heard the defence of this action. I had come from a situation where there were two Books in use, the *BCP* (1662) and the *Alternative Service Book* (1980). In the land of the free and in the Episcopal Church I found that freedom to be a traditional Anglican in public prayer worship and devotion was virtually forbidden. However, my spirits were raised as I gradually learned that thousands of laity and a few clergy felt as I did and quietly preserved the use of the *BCP* (1928) in parishes and homes.

I have often asked myself why it is that clergy of all kinds seem so committed to the *BCP* (1979) and generally support bishops who forbid the use of *BCP* (1928) in parishes. Two possible reasons come to mind. First of all this Book is a genuinely American book, produced by Americans for Americans after painful and long trial use. In contrast

BCP (1928) is only an American adaptation of a basically British (both English and Scottish) Book. Thus there is a sense of pride in this all-American production, which was published before the new English *ASB* (1980), and which may still claim to be the best of the new type of modern Anglican books of services.

In the second place, this Book is comprehensive, in that it provides for, and reflects in its contents and arrangement, a new pluralism. This provision fits well into a complex society such as America now is, satisfying at a symbolic level a felt religious need to provide for the individual parish but to affirm some unity of the whole denomination. Thus the Book has both traditional and modern language liturgies, with a decided bias towards the modern: in fact it surprised and pleased many Anglo-Catholic priests and parishes by incorporating as options most of their long standing demands (e.g. the Easter Vigil, provisions for the Reserved Sacrament and auricular Confession). Further, it gives vast scope for choice in what is used or not used in the services and, with respect to the Lord's Supper or Eucharist, it presents not one but six Eucharistic Prayers from which to choose. Then also it seems to avoid that concentration on sin, atonement and justification, on account of which vocal critics had long judged the *BCP* (1928) as being glued to older theology.

Faced with this breadth and these possibilities, how could any reasonable person oppose or not use such a Book! Those who cry out for the *BCP* (1928) ought to realize (it has often been said), that Rite I of the new Book provides for their needs. Thus let them leave the past and cease to bury their heads in the sand and enter into the modern experiment - otherwise they will get left behind. (The defence and commendation of the Common Prayer Tradition, as represented in the *BCP* (1928), will be offered throughout this book by a cumulative argument concerning the nature of Common Prayer, the priority of Holy Scripture, and the nature of Catholic dogma.)

Second shock

The second shock came upon me gradually and it began at the General Convention of the Episcopal Church at Phoenix in July, 1991. It was as a result of the realization that there is an equating of the *zeitgeist* (spirit of the age) with the Holy Spirit by much of the leadership of the Church. The nature of the Holy Spirit, as the Spirit of Christ, is presented in Scripture for our study and meditation in such places as John 14-16 and Romans 8. He is the Spirit of holiness and wholeness, of regeneration and renewal, of goodness and faithfulness, and He leads us in the way of Christ. What He guides disciples of Jesus to be and to do stands in contrast and opposition to the secular spirit of the world, the raw desires of the flesh and the temptations of the devil. The Holy Spirit is on no account to be confused with the spirit of the age or the modern spirit - however this contemporary spirit is defined. I have been profoundly disturbed to hear of such things as the right of human beings to name God as they choose, and the practice of homosexuality and lesbianism, described as examples of the way the Holy Spirit is showing us new values and truths today. Is this not coming near to that sin our Lord said was not forgivable - sin against the Holy Spirit? (See Matt. 12:31; Mark 3:29; Luke 12:10.)

As I shall explain in the next two chapters this confusion of the Person of the Holy Spirit with the modern, secular spirit is in part possible because of the various doctrines of God being taught in the Church. These are of such a nature that they give great emphasis to the immanence and omnipresence of God as Spirit and little if any emphasis to the utter transcendence of God, apart from and above the created order. If God is reduced to the cosmos then it is only a short step to identifying cultural and historical movement as the expression of God as Spirit.

Third shock

The third shock which also came upon me slowly rather than suddenly was to discover just how deeply the liberal or modernist agenda has penetrated the process of liturgical revision since the 1970s. In fact the whole Liturgical Movement which began with good intentions seems to have gone off course and to have become the vanguard for the revision of the Faith through the revision of the services we use. It is to be seen in the way in which *BCP* (1979) and the Canadian *BAS* (1985) are being used (e.g. the rubric allowing the omission of the confession of sins being taken as a rule always to omit confession of sins, or to omit the confession for the fifty days following Easter), but also in the plans for further and more radical revised services (to which *Prayer Book Studies 30*, with its inclusive language liturgies, points).

I recall how concerned C.S.Lewis was about the moves in England to update the Liturgy and wrote:

I would ask the clergy to believe that we, laymen, are more interested in orthodoxy and less interested in liturgiology as such than they can easily imagine... What we laymen fear is that the deepest doctrinal issues should be tacitly and implicitly settled by what seem to be, merely changes in liturgy. A man who is wondering whether the fare set before him is food or poison is not reassured by being told that the course is now restored to its traditional place in the menu or that the tureen is of the Sarum [i.e. old Salisbury] pattern. We laymen are ignorant and timid. Our lives are ever in our hands, the avenger of blood is on our heels and of each of us his soul may this night be required. Can you blame us if the reduction of grave doctrinal issues to merely liturgical issues fills us with something like terror? (*God in the Dock*, 1970, p.332.)

On the next page Professor Lewis has a further word on the relation of liturgy and belief. "I submit that the relation is healthy when liturgy expresses the belief of the Church, morbid when liturgy creates in the people by suggestion beliefs which the Church has not publicly professed, taught and believed." As we go on our journey in this book (especially chapter ten) we shall notice some of these grave doctrinal issues being covered up through claims that the new *lex orandi is the new lex credendi* (the new law of prayer is the new law of faith, for which see chapter 10).

I also recall the words of the late W. H. Auden, who took part in some of the early work on revising the Psalter in the 1960s. He saw a wonderful tradition of prayer-language slipping away in the euphoria of revision and wrote in his Commonplace Book:

> The Episcopal Church...seems to have gone stark, raving mad... And why? The Roman Catholics [after Vatican II] have had to start from scratch, and as any of them with a feeling for language will admit, they have made a cacophonous horror of the mass. Whereas we had the extraordinary good fortune in that our Prayer Book was composed at exactly the right historical moment. The English language had already become more or less what it is today...but the ecclesiastics of the 16th century still possessed a feeling for the ritual and ceremonious which today we have almost certainly lost. (*A Certain World*, 1970, p.85.)

My concern is primarily with the doctrine and spirituality but I fully recognize that these must be expressed in excellent English.

My purpose in writing

Therefore I write this book as a way of saying that I am an Anglican, that I want to be a biblical and catholic Anglican, and that I see no hope of being an honest Anglican only within the context provided by further developments of the revisionist tradition of liturgy contained in the *BCP* (1979) and the *BAS* (1985). Therefore the witness of the Prayer Book Societies in the USA, Canada, England and elsewhere is necessary. Classic Anglicanism in which sacred Scripture has central place, and where truly Common Prayer, with its unique asceticism and spirituality arising from the prayerful reading of Scripture and receiving of Holy Communion, must not be allowed to disappear for want of effort!

If I were asked for a biblical text to set forth what I have to say, I would choose the word of the Lord through the prophet, Jeremiah. "Stand ye in the ways, and see, and ask for the old paths, where is the good way, and walk therein, and ye shall find rest for your souls" (6:16). I call upon Anglicans to survey the history and experience of the Churches to which they belong, to contemplate and think seriously about the Common Prayer Tradition, and then to compare the old with the new. I hope they will choose the old way, not to bury their heads in the sands of the past but with the intention of working to see its perfection for the Anglican Way for today and tomorrow. For, in the new way upon which parts of the Anglican Communion are travelling I do not see any long-term "rest for souls."

At the moment it is just possible, I believe, by the judicious use of the new Books to be an Anglican in terms of biblical faith and public worship; but the process of revision which seems only to have just started will surely make that possibility an impossibility soon - unless a halt is called to further revision and doctrinal change, and unless we put the whole process into some kind of reverse gear, by rediscovering the primacy of biblical faith.

My pessimism concerning the new mix-and-match tradition in modern Anglicanism stands in contrast to that confidence which once was so widespread with respect to the Common Prayer Tradition. Here is what J.P.K. Henshaw, Bishop of Rhode Island wrote in 1831:

Among the many causes of gratitude to Almighty God which distinguish our lot as Protestant Episcopalians, it is not one of the least that we are favored with a scriptural and established LITURGY; which is entitled to the warmest commendation, not only as a directory for public worship, but also as a standard and preservative of sound doctrine.

The Prayer Book has been beautifully and appropriately styled "the daughter of the Bible"; and, probably, there is no other work of human composition which has embodied so much of the substance and spirit of the heavenly Oracles. Extracts from the Bible, in the form of Gospels, Epistles and Psalter, constitute the greater part of the volume - and throughout the collects and prayers the spirit of the divine Word breathes and glows and animates the whole. What can be more chaste and spiritual than its devotional services? What more humble and meek than its penitential confessions? What more fervent and comprehensive than its acts of intercession? What more full, ardent and seraphic than its adorations and thanksgivings? How many of the followers of Christ in this day have felt their hearts glow with heavenly ardor - as if touched with a live coal from the altar - and experienced the sublime delights of spiritual communion in the use of those prayers and praises in which saints and martyrs of every age have poured forth their devotions to the Lord? And eternity only can disclose the multitude of instances in which the use of them has alleviated the pains of disease, assuaged the fears of the mariner amidst the terrors of the ocean, cheered the desolations of prison and softened the bed of death.

The LITURGY is entitled to veneration not only as a devotional work but as a compendium of sound Christian theology. All the fundamental and important doctrines of the Gospel are interwoven throughout its various offices; and while our congregations statedly use it they will be secured against the introduction of gross and flagrant heresy. (*The Communicant's Guide*, 1831, p.3.)

The Bishop goes on to speak of the "Order for the administration of the Lord's Supper" as being nothing less than the condensing of "the excellencies of the ancient liturgies" into a wonderful English liturgy.

In this book I shall be saying something similar to what Bishop Henshaw and many others have said about the Common Prayer Tradition, but with less eloquence. However, my primary interest is in showing that a major purpose of Common Prayer is to enable believing sinners to know God in a personal way through corporate worship.

Our God is the LORD and we are made in His image and after His likeness to be His adoring creatures not only in this age but for all eternity. Therefore to begin to know Him now in corporate worship is to prepare to know Him in heaven in the Liturgy of the angels and saints.

[*Note.* To those who wish to reflect further upon the religious, liturgical and theological divide in the Episcopal Church (as well in other similiar American Churches) I commend James Davidson Hunter, *Culture Wars: The Struggle to Define America*, Basic Books, 1991.]

2

LITURGY SINCE CRANMER

The tradition of an English Book of Common Prayer began in 1549 and passed through important new editions in 1552 and 1662 in England, with later revised editions in the English-speaking world of the British Empire and the nations which evolved from it. There were of course editions in foreign languages as well, especially for churches founded by missionary endeavor. In North America the last revised editions which embodied this Common Prayer Tradition were those of 1928 in the USA and 1962 in Canada. Because of this shared tradition by world-wide Anglicanism it was possible until fairly recently to go to Anglican worship anywhere in the world and soon feel at home with the forms of divine service.

In the 1990s we are experiencing a growing variety of forms of worship not only in different countries but also within countries. This variety is usually based upon author-ized books of prayer which still use the title or claim the concept of "Common Prayer" (e.g. *The Book of Common Prayer*, 1979, in the USA and *The Alternative Service Book, 1985,* in Canada). However, these Books of varying titles have begun a new tradition of public worship and prayer for Anglicanism not only in North America but also around the world (cf. the *ASB*, 1980, in England).

Their creators have often claimed and still claim to be restoring valuable ancient forms and ways to modern wor-ship without changing the basic doctrine. However, their primary thrust seems to be that of encouraging a seemingly endless variety of possibilities into divine worship and thereby introducing a dull mediocrity into worship. In this way they claim to speak to contemporary persons in modern language. Gone is one excellent form of words and in its place are several alternatives, none of which is aesthetically memorable or theologically satisfying. Gone also is the clarity of biblical and patristic teaching on fundamental matters and in its place is at best a fuzzy or careless presentation of certain basic doctrines. Further, while it is argued that this modern way involves the participation of the laity (as the people of God) in worship much more than was the case in former years, the usual position in practice is that the priest becomes the expert to choose between the variety of possible forms of service in the Book.

Solid Foundation

Of course I am not claiming that the classic tradition of Anglican Common Prayer was or is perfect. I am not saying that the American *BCP* (1928) and Canadian *BCP* (1962) would not benefit from some wise and gentle revision and from a new preface to explain the logic of saving and sanctifying faith on which this type of worship is based and from which it proceeds. It is possible that some of the new services introduced into the recent Prayer Books (e.g. Easter services) could be incorporated, adapting them to the theology and ethos of the Common Prayer Tradition. Then provision could be made for the use of a revised Psalter, the kind, for example, authorized in England in 1966, and called *The Revised Psalter*, which had both C.S.Lewis and T.S.Eliot on its revision committee.

However, the major point is that the Books of 1928 and 1962 can be improved or their contents adjusted for contemporary use because their basic tradition is sound and well tried in all important respects. Since the foundation is solid there is possibility for a limited number of optional additions here and there as long as they are done in the same ethos and doctrine as the original. The grandeur and glory of the tradition of Common Prayer is that there has been a shared, excellent form of worship to be used by all who belong to a particular branch of Christendom - in this case the Anglican

Way. The excellence is not only in the form of words but also in the way this tradition reflects the ethos and doctrine of Holy Scripture as well as the classic, patristic, Trinitarian doctrinal and devotional heritage of the one, holy, catholic and apostolic Church.

In contrast, the *BCP* (1979) and the *BAS* (1985) were intended, at least by some of their advocates, to create a different and opposed tradition of Christian worship. In justice, they may be called revisionist Books for, if widely or universally used, their impact will be to destroy the received, classic tradition of Common Prayer which has been at the very center of the genius of Anglicanism. In fact this destruction is well advanced already in North America, since a generation now exists for whom the tradition of authentic Common Prayer has not been a living experience.

Shaky Foundation

The charge that these new Books are revisionist can be substantiated on three major grounds. First of all, as we have been noting, they introduce a new concept and practice of public worship. Out of the church door goes a common or shared form and in the door comes a variety which is only intended to be a stage on the way to more variety. Already Liturgical Commissions have produced and even now they continue to produce more experimental forms of public worship. Soon there will be only a loose-leaf book of possible options.

One important development since 1979 has been the move to produce services based on the principle of inclusivism with non-excluding language. Already in the Psalter of *BCP* (1979) this principle had been utilized, but *Prayer Book Studies 30* (1990), given further limited approval by the General Convention of 1991, is an example of this novelty: with the continuing trial use of its inclusivist liturgies a further nail is hammered into the coffin of the Common Prayer Tradition and in the authority of Holy Scripture in the Church. For, if God be the LORD who reveals Himself to us through the words of Scripture, then God may be said to name Himself: as mere sinful creatures we cannot choose to name Him but we address Him after His own self-naming and direction. I shall return to this theme in chapter eleven below.

In the second place, there is a definite weakening of basic Christian doctrine in the new Books. In fact it is not claiming too much to say that there is evidence of a definite move to revise Christian doctrine in some places within them. One does not have to look very far with a trained eye to see that the doctrines of the Holy Trinity, the glorious Person and saving Work of our Lord Jesus Christ, and the nature of God's salvation have all been either modified or revised. Many good and faithful Episcopalians have not noticed this doctrinal change because they have in charity assumed that the *BCP* (1979) has the same doctrine as that of the *BCP* (1928) and have read classical doctrine into the words they have read.

Take for example the doctrine of the Trinity. This doctrine has been preserved in the old form in the *Gloria* ("Glory be to the Father..." etc) used at the end of the Canticles and Psalms in the *BCP* (1979) as well as in the Blessing, given at the end of public worship by the bishop or priest. It has been lost, however, in other places, most obviously in the opening Blessing of God in Rites I and II of the Eucharist. Instead of "Blessed be God: the Father, the Son and the Holy Spirit" (for our God is One God in Three Persons) we are given a formula which is a form of the ancient heresy of Modalism (God is One but has three names). The definite articles are left out and thus instead of "the Father, the Son and the Holy Spirit" we are given "Father, Son and Holy Spirit".

Another obvious example of change is in the use of a revised form of the Apostles' Creed. Though in the original Latin and in the long-used English translation the virginal conception of our Lord is clearly set forth in the words, "He was conceived by the Holy Spirit and born of the Virgin Mary," the revised form in Morning Prayer Rite II has the words "He was conceived by the power of the Holy Spirit and born of the Virgin Mary." The aim of the new words is to allow people who do not believe in the miraculous conception of Jesus to think of His conception as if it were like that of Isaac or John the Baptist—normal but special. Such an interpretation is, of course, heresy. In fact, as you survey the theological content of the *BCP* (1979) you notice a general tendency to treat and present Jesus as the Perfect Man in whom the divine presence dwells. That is, He becomes for all of us a supreme example of God's presence and as well of our response to God in faith. To think of Jesus only as a revelation of God and as a perfect example to us is surely something short of confessing Him as "my Lord and my God."

Further changes are made later in the Apostles' Creed when the "descent into hell" is made into another less important journey ("a descent to the dead") and the adjective "almighty" which follows "right hand of the Father" is omitted. Then serious changes are made to the translation of the Nicene Creed as that is printed in Rite II of the Eucharist (and taken from the International Commission on Liturgical Texts). I urge my readers to compare the old translation "I believe..." with the new one "We believe..." in Rites I and II. There are so many significant changes and it is inappropriate to examine them all here. I simply note that to say "we believe" is not the same as saying "I believe". We are there together at Holy Communion as the Body of Christ and each believer who is present is a member of that Body: thus each of us has to respond to the God who has revealed and given Himself to us: therefore, the right response is "Lord, I believe!" Though the members of the Council of Nicea composed the Creed and said together against heretics, "We [as a body standing together] believe" they each confessed the same faith in the Eucharist in personal terms, "I believe" (as the ancient Liturgies of St Basil and St Chrysostom show).

Thirdly, there is a definite change in the doctrine and use of the Bible. Take, for example, the translation of Psalms 1:1 and 51:6 in the Psalter of 1928 and 1962 on the one hand and that of 1979 and 1985 on the other. In 1:1 the original speaks of the blessed man (male and singular): this is faithfully translated by the old Psalter and by the Revised Standard Version and other versions of the Bible; but, in the American 1979 and the Canadian 1985 Psalters (which are virtually identical) we have a third person neuter, "happy are they..." To make matters worse there is no note anywhere in the American 1979 Psalter to let the faithful know that they have been given an inclusivist translation which is informed by the ideology of anti-sexism. In contrast, the Canadian Psalter does have a preface which recognizes the inclusivist nature of the translation and allows the use of other versions.

Then if you compare Psalm 51 in the old and new translations you find that the full extent of the nature of sin is diminished in the 1979 Psalter. The human condition of sin as inherited from others and then personally exercised, is replaced in 1979 by a notion of individual freedom of choice as exercised only from one's mother's womb. Regrettably this diminution of the nature of sin harmonizes with the reduced doctrine of sin presented in the rest of the Books.

The Lectionary which accompanies *BCP* (1979) has certain attractive features to it but it also has some pernicious aspects. There is a selective dropping of those sections of Scripture which obviously stand in definite opposition to the insights of the revised religion - this is particularly so with respect to the Letters of Paul. Where the modern mind judges him to be passing on rabbinic rather than specifically Christian teaching on the relation between the male and female or the immorality of the practice of homosexuality then that rabbinic teaching is left out (see e.g. the omission of parts of Romans 1 and 1 Corinthians 11 & 14).

To some people the above examples of revision of doctrine may appear trivial and of little consequence. Yet to those who are familiar with the history of Christian doctrine and spirituality they do represent important changes or deviations which will have evangelistic and pastoral repercussions. Therefore if truth means anything at all these changes must be made explicit by those who care for truth.

Old but excellent

My primary purpose is not to attack the new approach to and ways of worship which the Anglican Communion is being increasingly led to experience through its new Books of Prayer. Rather it is to show that the old tradition of Common Prayer, despite its seemingly old-fashioned look, is an excellent way to know God, the living God, the God and Father of our Lord Jesus Christ, in public worship; further it is to recognize that from this knowing, trusting, and loving Him comes the serving and obeying of Him in daily life. However, to develop my theme and substantiate my arguments it will be necessary from time to time to contrast the old and the new ways; thus there will be some further criticism of the new ways. I do not apologize for this. It is unavoidable if it be the case that the modern way (as I have come to see it) is in fact truly inferior as a spiritual offering and sacrifice to God in holy worship. My concern is that at the level of revealed truth and devotion there be genuine knowing of God as our Father and Saviour.

The seeking after God and the knowledge of Him is the most deeply fulfilling journey upon which we can embark. We need a sure road to travel on, an accurate map to use and a faithful guide to direct us in our search for the living God and fellowship with Him. I believe that wise people will take that road, use that map and employ that guide which have proved themselves over the centuries to achieve what they promise. Modern forms of transport may be better than older ones: modern houses may be warmer than older ones; but, knowing God is not like using transport or buying houses. In this human quest we need to pay attention to the accumulated wisdom and tested practice of the centuries: this is more likely to lead us where we want to go than are modern insights and untested ways.

While the old way necessarily bears traces of the historical and cultural situation in which it was first put together, it has been so pruned and finely tuned over the centuries that it has achieved the position of being immediately adaptable and available to people who wish to take the call to Christian prayer seriously.

My plan for this book is governed by two major considerations. First, I want to strengthen the commitment of those who now use the *BCP* (1928 or 1962) and, secondly, I desire to encourage people who have not used a classic *BCP* to use one for the first time, if not in public then for their personal prayer and devotion. Then there are also those who probably once used it and, being overtaken by the new ways, ceased to use it. I hope they will pick up where they left off and do so with enthusiasm. Therefore I seek to explain first of all what is unique about knowing God and how this knowledge can only truly be received and experienced in a Liturgy where there is faithfulness to the God and Father of our Lord Jesus Christ and to His self-revelation recorded in Holy Scripture.

Having shown what it is to know God both personally and corporately, I proceed to comment on the major services and provisions of the Common Prayer Tradition in order to show how the knowing of God is presented and achieved in each (e.g. through saying Daily Prayer, reading Holy Scripture, receiving Holy Communion on the Lord's Day and participating in the Church Year). Finally, I offer my thoughts on such topics as inclusive language and the doctrinal content of knowing the Lord our God.

Through this process I show that Liturgy (the corporate worship of Almighty God through written services of worship for Baptism, Confirmation, Daily Prayer and Holy Communion) is truly the work (*ergon*) which the *laos* (people) of God do before God. Liturgy has to do with people and work - God's believing people engaged in God's holy work, the work He has called them to offer to Him. In Hebrews 8:6 the word liturgy is used of what Jesus Christ Himself is now doing for His Church in heaven before the Father: "Christ has obtained a ministry [liturgy-*leitourgia*] which is as much more excellent than the old ministry [of the high priest] as the covenant He mediates is better [than the old Mosaic covenant], since it is enacted on better promises." The Church at worship is united within the new covenant to the liturgy of Christ, His precious death and glorious resurrection, His ascension into heaven and His ministry there as our King, High Priest and Prophet. In the Common Prayer Tradition this union with Christ is expected, anticipated and wonderfully achieved by the grace of God; and to this, I believe, millions in the Church Expectant or Triumphant now testify! Thanks be to God.

All in all my aim is to show that by God's good providence there is within the Common Prayer Tradition a logic of faith, derived from the New Testament. This is intended to operate both corporately in God's people gathered as Christ's Body and in individual persons in their relationship with God through Jesus Christ. If this logic of faith is disturbed or, worse still, repudiated, then the Common Prayer Tradition as a biblical tradition is lost and great, maybe irreprable, harm done to the Anglican Way.

3

WHAT KNOWING IS

Our subject is an exalted one—knowing God, the LORD, Himself, not His creatures but knowing Him, our Creator and Redeemer. In what we call His high priestly prayer Jesus prayed that they (His disciples) "might know thee, the only true God" (John 17:3). To know the heavenly Father is the highest of privileges and the greatest of experiences. In order to begin to understand what such knowing is all about we need first of all to spend a little time reflecting upon what we mean when we claim, "I know him or her" or " I know this or that thing."

Knowing persons

To know my next-door neighbor is a more complex business than to know a place, book, language or even an animal. I can know a book or a language through learning it and a place such as Pikes Peak in Colorado by visiting and climbing it. I can know a dog by being its owner over a period of time and exercising, feeding, training and being dependent upon it. If it were as easy to know human persons as it is to know things and animals the world would probably be a different place!

I believe that there is a tendency in all of us to boast about important people with whom we have been acquainted. For example, I might claim in a conversation, "I know Margaret Thatcher." This claim could be based on my living on the same street as she did and having had several conversations with her over the garden wall. Or you might claim that you know President Bush because you belonged to the same social club as he did twenty years ago and chatted with him at the bar.

When we speak of knowing a person we may be referring to minimal or maximum knowledge of him or her for there are degrees and depths of knowledge of persons. For example, I know about a lot of people through watching them on the TV screen and seeing their pictures and profiles in the newspapers and magazines. I know what they look like, how they speak and what kinds of things they do in their career and public lives. With few, if any, of these people do I have any personal relationship. I merely know about them. And even if what I know about them is a lot, it is still the case that I only know about them. Though I may feel I know one or two of them in a personal way the truth of the matter is that I really and truly only know about them for I have no personal relationship with any of them.

Further, I can say much the same about most of the people I meet day by day at places where I work, enjoy leisure and do my shopping. This also probably applies to most people in my church. Certainly I may know a lot about some of them for I may carefully study their personality, facial expressions, words, dress, relationships and lifestyles; but, it remains true that I only know about them.

However, there are certain persons whom I really know. Not only do I know about them but I have such a personal relationship with them that I actually do truly know them rather than merely know about them. This is possible because each of them has in different ways and by various means disclosed his or her inner life, thoughts and being to me. Usually this personal knowing works both ways through friendship or within family ties or in happy marriage. You reveal yourself to me and I open up myself to you - not all at once but gradually and as circumstances allow. However, it can be the case that I as a pastor am allowed to know a person because he or she has freely disclosed his or her inner life confidentially to me in order to seek my help.

Who is God?

When we speak of knowing God we have in mind, I think, both knowing about Him and knowing Him in personal friendship. We need to know something about God, Creator and Redeemer, in order to accept His gracious call to enter a personal relationship of faith in Him and love of Him. However, if we take the "Ministration of Holy Baptism" seriously then we must rejoice in the fact that God places infants in a right relationship with Himself from the time of their baptism. Then within this growing personal friendship with the Lord in the fellowship of the church the child learns about this God in whom he trusts.

Let us first reflect upon what it is to know about God. As Anglicans and Episcopalians our knowledge of God is the same as that of the whole Church, Eastern and Western, Catholic and Protestant, for we all trace our history back to the same source, the apostolic Church. This knowledge is given the technical name of "classical Christian theism" by theologians in order to distinguish it from other ways of stating a claimed knowledge of God. For example, we do not accept the ever-popular doctrine of pantheism, the doctrine that God is equivalent to nature and that the natural order is either God or the external expression of God. There have always been pantheists in western culture, poets like Walt Whitman for example. Anglicans who take their Bible and Prayer Book seriously do not believe that God is the equivalent of nature. They confess that He is the Lord of nature.

Further, we do not accept deism, a doctrine of God popular in the eighteenth century both in America and Europe, and intimately associated with the Enlightenment. Deism is the teaching that God created the world and then left it all alone to get on with its existence. That is, like a great clockmaker, He made a clock and then wound it up to let it get on with the job of keeping time. Rejecting this approach Anglicans believe that God the Creator is also God the Sustainer and Redeemer: God cares for the world that He made *ex nihilo* (out of nothing); and by His mighty word He keeps it in existence and order moment by moment. This belief is expressed often through the use of the Psalter in the Daily Office (e.g. Ps.29), as well as in the Canticle, *Venite*, at Morning Prayer. So what is theism? It is the belief in one God who is the Creator of the world; He is infinite, self-existent, incorporeal, eternal, immutable, impassible, simple, omniscient and omnipotent. These words are here used in their technical or philosophical meaning. A shorter answer is to say that God is a Spirit, infinite, eternal, and unchangeable in His being, wisdom, power, holiness, justice, goodness and truth. A simpler way to answer the question is to say that theism is belief in one God who totally transcends (is above and wholly distinct from) the world that He made and who is perfect in wisdom, power and love.

Historically the two chief rivals to theism have been polytheism (the belief in many gods, as in ancient Rome and Greece and in popular Hinduism today) and pantheism (the view that the world itself is divine because it is the self-expression of God's very being). Today there is also a sophisticated form of pantheism called panentheism which teaches that the self-development of God is inextricably connected with the evolution of the universe. This is usually expressed through the process philosophy of the late A.N.Whitehead which sees God as constantly changing and growing in perfection through including within His being the experiences of the world - which may be called "God's body" (as in some feminist theology).

Deism, to which we referred above, is a rational form of theism and still is accepted and/or taught by those who do not think that God actually involves Himself in or acts within the world. It is probably fair to say that some old-style biblical scholars who reject the intervention of God through miracles are deists. (Do you remember the collection of essays entitled *The Myth of God Incarnate*, published in 1977 ? Much of the thought in that book arose from or was an expression of deism. See, further, David Brown, *The Divine Trinity*, 1985, pp. 3-50.)

Modern living forms of theism include Judaism and Islam. There is of course a profound continuity between Jewish and Christian theism for the first disciples were Jewish theists who were wholly committed to the LORD, their God. Yet, through their encounter with Jesus, they eventually went forth gladly and commitedly to baptize converts to Christianity "in the name of the Father, the Son and the Holy Spirit." They moved from the confession of One God to the confession of One God in Trinity.

Therefore what distinguishes classical Christian theism from any other form of theism is that Christians believe, teach and confess that God eternally exists not only as the One and Only God but as One God in Three Persons—the Father, the Son and the Holy Spirit. Further, Christians also hold that the eternal Son became incarnate as Jesus, the Christ, and that He alone is the means of their salvation. Thus it may rightly be claimed that the "extra" beliefs concerning God which Christians hold and Jews do not share are based wholly on divine revelation, as that is received in and through Jesus Himself. The confession that Jesus is Lord and that Jesus is the Son of God incarnate lead on in the life of the Church to the confession that the eternal God is One God in Three Persons. Under the general guidance of the Holy Spirit Christian experience of God in worship and in daily life, together with reflection upon the teaching of Jesus and the apostles, led to the doctrine of the Trinity. The doctrine arose to explain the vital, spiritual and moral experience of God within the fellowship of Christians, for the Church knew and worshipped the Father through the Son in the Holy Spirit.

Of course the confession of the Holy Trinity has to be stated with great care for it can be so easily misunderstood. For example, it can be carelessly stated and taken to mean that God is One God with three major names (Father, Son and Spirit)—this was called Modalism or Sabellianism in the Early Church. (Regrettably this error seems to have entered into the *BCP* 1979 at several significant places—e.g. the opening Blessing of the Eucharist in Rites I & II.) Or the Trinity can be taken to mean that there are three equal Gods called the Father, the Son and the Holy Spirit. This is tritheism. Then there is the concept of the Trinity as a descending hierarchy of three related but not equal expressions of deity. First is the Father; at a lower level of deity is the Son and at an even lower level is the Holy Spirit. Thus only the Father is really God - the Son and the Spirit are superior angels. The fact that these pitfalls are there ought to cause us to be thankful that the doctrine of the Holy Trinity is stated with great care and accuracy in the Common Prayer Tradition, especially where that contains the *Quicunque Vult,* or *The Athanasian Creed.*

A typical Anglican devotion for Trinity Sunday will be something like this:

Come let us adore the Sacred Trinity, Three Persons and One God.

To Thee, the eternal Father, made by none;

To Thee, the increated Son, begotten by the Father alone;

To Thee, the blessed Spirit, proceeding from the Father and the Son;

To this one, holy, consubstantial and undivided Trinity, be ascribed all power and wisdom and glory, now and for ever.

Holy, holy, holy, Lord God of Sabaoth.

Heaven and earth are full of the Majesty of thy glory.

Further, the constant appearance of heresies and errors ought to make us keen to learn sound and edifying knowledge about the God whom we worship.

The living God

There is much to know about God, for He is like a glorious, everlastingly inexhaustible Fountain from which we drink and continue to drink. He is super-essential Being and the more we know about Him the more we realize that there is to know. Knowledge of the LORD as the Holy Trinity is fundamental and without this knowledge we can make no progress in worship and devotion; but, there are many other aspects to the knowledge of God that we need to know in order that we might grow in our personal relationship with Him.

For this reason we study and meditate upon the Holy Scriptures. Anglicans have always claimed that the Scriptures of the Old and New Testament are the first source of our knowledge of God. For the Anglican who devoutly follows and uses the Lectionary there is a daily immersion in the vital source of our knowledge of the Lord our God. Further, the major aspects of the whole doctrine of God as that is provided in the Bible are woven into the wording of the various services provided in the Common Prayer tradition. For example, the teaching that God is the dynamic Creator and Sustainer of the universe and that by His providence He works all things for the purpose of His glory is clearly and reverentially stated in the Collects and Prayers.

Over the centuries Christians have learned about God from being taught the Creed and the Catechism, by hearing and reading the Bible, and by accepting the teaching about God which appears in the text of the Prayer Book. This has been augmented by sermons, by further teaching, by home study groups and personal study and reflection. In the daily services of Morning and Evening Prayer there is the requirement that the participants confess their faith in the words of the Apostles' Creed—" I believe in God the Father almighty..." In the Order for Holy Communion there is also the requirement that the Nicene or the Apostles' Creed be used. The Nicene, like the Apostles', begins in a personal way "I believe in one God.." and goes on to state with a marvelous economy of words what I called above, classical Christian theism - Trinitarian Theism. There is yet a further official confession of faith in Anglicanism which fell into disuse from the eighteenth century onwards in America but which is, to my mind, a moving and succinct statement of the doctrine of the Trinity and the doctrine of the Person of Christ. I referred to it above as the *Quicunque Vult* or the *Athanasian Creed*: it has an integral place in the *BCP* (1662) of the Church of England.

In saying "I believe..." each Christian present is speaking for himself and stating the faith of the Church. It is a confession that points not only to knowledge and beliefs about God but also to a truly personal relation with God the Father through God the Incarnate Son. The Creed may be seen as the response of the believer to the revelation of and salvation from God in Jesus Christ given to each of us. On the basis of what God has said and done, I say to Him, "Lord I believe..." Thus something of importance is lost in modern Anglican services where the Creed begins, "We believe..."

This Trinitarian Theism expressed in the Nicene Creed informs the whole approach to and content of worship. Even though it is only stated explicitly here and there (e.g. in the *Gloria* at the end of the singing or recital of each psalm and in the final Blessing) the knowledge of God the Holy Trinity is present as the great unifying doctrine and dogma of the whole Common Prayer Tradition. Knowledge about God is intended to be the expression of personal knowing of God in the services of worship, be they the Daily Office or the Administration of the Sacraments of Baptism and Holy Communion. We are to worship the Father through and in the Son by and in the Holy Spirit. The trinitarian structure of the services therefore exists as the vehicle for our faith-knowledge of God as Holy Trinity so that we may both pray together and as individual persons in common (i.e. genuine communal) prayer. Joined to Christ Jesus in faith and through the Holy Spirit, we join in His prayer, which He offers perpetually for His brethren at the right hand of the Father (Rom.8:34). We lift up our hearts and through the Holy Spirit we are united to Him as our Mediator and High Priest. He is the Head and we are the members of His Body and therefore being in Him we are united to the Holy Trinity.

Almighty and everlasting God, who hast given unto us thy servants grace, by the confession of a true faith, to acknowledge the glory of the eternal Trinity, and in the power of the Divine Majesty to worship the Unity: We beseech thee, that thou wouldest keep us stedfast in this faith, and evermore defend us from all adversities, who livest and reignest one God, world without end. Amen.

In the words of the *Quicunque Vult*: "the Catholic Faith is this: That we worship one God in Trinity, and Trinity in Unity."

4

COVENANT WITH GOD

We need to take time now to reflect upon the nature of the relationship which we have with God since the way we understand this relationship will determine to a large measure our attitudes within common prayer and worship. If I come to common worship thinking that my relationship with God is that of an equal or near-equal partner with God then my attitude will reflect that mindset. If I come thinking that I am doing God some kind of favor or showing Him some special loyalty then my attitude will reflect this mindset. In contrast, if I come in gratitude and humility, conscious of my sins and unworthiness but overwhelmed by God's mercy to me in Jesus Christ then my attitude will be very different.

God's initiative

In the Bible God enters into a relationship with believing sinners through what is called His covenant. We tend to think of a covenant as an agreement or contract between two parties who are of the same kind or who are equal in some way or another. The Bible contains references to such covenants—e.g. agreements between kings. However, God's covenant with man is not an agreement between equals and it is not a contract to which both sides agree. It is a totally one-sided affair because God alone establishes it and in doing so He sets out its terms and conditions. Then to remind us of our sinful, creaturely status and reduce our pride God tells us that we can only fulfil the conditions of the covenant as His junior covenant partners with His help. In fact without the help of the Holy Spirit we cannot even enter, let alone live rightly within, His covenant.

On first consideration this may seem to be dictatorial and tyrannical action by God. Yet, if we take time to reflect upon such a covenant, we shall see that we are not talking of two equal partners but of the Lord God, the Creator and Sustainer of the universe, whom the angels serve and adore and who is infinitely above our being and our thought. He is God and we are mere creatures - sinful, spiritually and morally diseased creatures! Further, if we recognize that His covenant is truly a covenant of grace and is established for our good and eternal welfare that we may become His children and be restored to genuine knowing and loving of Him for all eternity, then we shall probably admit not only that He has every right to act as He has but that He has acted in mercy and compassion towards us by establishing His covenant of grace. For the simple fact is that we of ourselves cannot help ourselves in terms of lifting ourselves up to God in order to negotiate with Him. He must come towards us. His covenant of grace is His coming towards us so that we can draw near to Him.

The initiative and grace of God in our salvation is most clearly understood and presented in the *BCP* (1928), as in *BCP* (1962). The First Office of Instruction of the Catechism in *BCP* (1928) begins with this Collect:

Lord of all power and might, who art the author and giver of all good things; graft in our hearts the love of thy name, increase in us true religion, nourish us with all goodness, and of thy great mercy keep us in the same; through Jesus Christ our Lord. Amen.

It is also the Collect for the seventh Sunday after Trinity. Its words clearly point both to the initiative of God towards us and of His help to us in fulfilling our duties of His covenant. He is the "author" and "giver" and it is He alone who can "increase", "nourish" and "keep" His believing children in His grace and covenant. Our genuine freedom is to do His bidding with His gracious help.

In contrast the *BCP* (1979) does not have this clarity of commitment to the initiative and assistance of God in His relationship with His people. There is lurking there both in its Catechism (An Outline of the Faith) and in some of the Collects (e.g. that of the First Sunday after the Epiphany, which refers to the covenant as being made by those who are baptized!) the tendency to treat human beings as if they were negotiating, near-equal covenant partners with God! This tendency reflects, of course, the pride of modern man who refuses to recognize that he is not merely in rebellion against God (which *BCP* 1979 seems to teach) but that he is so sick and diseased by sin that he cannot truly help himself (which *BCP* 1979 appears to downplay or reject).

The biblical teaching

God's relationship with human beings is established and begins with His relationship of Creator to created. This can never change for, however ennobled man is, he can never be God. He will always be a finite and dependent and contingent being looking unto God in whom, as Paul declares, he lives and moves and has his being (Acts 17:28). However, within this relationship which man has marred by sinfulness and rebellion God has moved to establish a further relationship, a relationship of grace and unmerited favor, whose full content is a new creation.

The Lord God began this new relationship when He declared, "I will establish my covenant" (Gen.6:18; Ex.6:4-5). Then the essence of the covenant was captured by God's declaration: "I will take you to me for a people and I will be to you a God" (Ex.6:7; see also Gen.17:7 & Rev.21:2-3). The covenant is unilateral in origin and establishment: it is not only offered but it is given unto Abraham and his descendants. Thus it is two sided when it comes into practical effect for the recipients (Israel and then the Church) become by God's mercy and choice His covenant partners. He is to them their LORD and they are to worship, trust, love and obey Him as He directs (Deut. 7:9, 13; 1 Kings 8:23).

God established His covenant of grace with Abraham (Gen.17:7) and his descendants. On Mount Sinai a special administration of this covenant was established with Israel through Moses (see Ex. 19ff.). In the Five Books of Moses (Genesis to Deuteronomy) we learn not only of what God's initiative and relationship meant but also what were the covenant obligations of the people of Israel. While God promised to be the living God who would guide, protect and bless them and care for them as His elect people, they in turn were committed to be His people on His terms and according to His conditions. In their relationship to Him there were no negotiating possibilities for He was their God who brought them up out of the land of Egypt and who would lead them into the promised land. The Ten Commandments began with a statement of faith - the God who commands is the living God who has redeemed and will guide His people (see Ex.20:1-2).

In the rest of the Old Testament (= Old Covenant) we read both of God's continuing faithfulness to His elect people and of their imperfect response to His gracious mercy and guidance. The story of the Books of Samuel, Kings and Chronicles is the story more of failure to be His faithful covenant partners than of success in that vocation. Much of what the prophets declared was a word from heaven calling upon the Israelites to fulfil their covenantal duties. The people were called to know their Lord God and in knowing Him to reject other gods; but so often they chose not to know Him and to go after Baal and the gods of Canaan. Yet, despite their apostasy and pride, God, Yahweh (Jehovah) remained their God never forgetting them.

Speaking through Jeremiah the Lord God addressed His covenant people in these words:

Let not the wise man glory in his wisdom, neither let the mighty man glory in his might, let not the rich man glory in his riches; but let him that glorieth glory in this, that he understands and knoweth me, that I am the LORD which exercise loving-kindness, judgment, and righteousness in the earth; for in these I delight (9:23-24).

The LORD delights to see in His creatures a true knowledge of Himself. Through Hosea He said: "For I desired mercy and not sacrifice; and the knowledge of God more than burnt offerings" (6:6). Within the Mosaic covenant what God looked for in and through the use of the Temple, the sacrificial system and priesthood was a people who knew Him and thus worshipped from within knowledge.

With the Incarnation of the eternally begotten Son of God, the Word made flesh, God revealed the length and breadth, height and depth, of His mercy and of His covenant of grace. In and through Jesus Christ, God the Father established what Jesus Himself called "a new covenant" (see Matt. 26:26-30) - the fullness of His covenant of grace. In the atoning, reconciling work of Jesus, God made possible for people of all races and all times what He had offered and given to Israel in a limited space and time. By His sacrificial death and shed blood Jesus established the covenant of grace on new foundations. He became the Mediator through whom believing sinners come to God and call Him "Father".

Jesus Christ is now the Way, the Truth and the Life and no-one comes to the Father except through Him. And those who come in faith to the Father in and through Him are not only adopted as the children of God but also in their souls God deigns to dwell as He promised through Jeremiah, the prophet. " Behold... I will make a new covenant... I will put my law in their inward parts and write it in their hearts; and I will be their God and they shall be my people... They shall all know me from the least of them unto the greatest of them" (31:31-34). This is not merely knowing about God but it is the knowing through direct communion with God in personal prayer and trusting relationship.

Anyone who carefully reads the New Testament (the account of how the new covenant was established by God the Father through God the Son by God the Holy Spirit) must see and understand that the relationship with God through faith and by the agency of the Holy Spirit is genuinely personal and dynamic. It is a relationship which operates in both directions with the human movement to God through Jesus Christ being always dependent upon His primary movement through Jesus Christ and in the Holy Spirit to His children. Within this covenant God calls His people into ever deepening fellowship, union and communion with Himself for He delights to be known by His redeemed creatures. Has he not made them in order that they might enjoy and love Him forever? Human knowing of God begins in personal and corporate prayer but it is extended from prayer into the whole of life, for God calls His people to walk with Him and to be aware everywhere and at all times of His presence with them. Paul himself wrote of knowing God in his sufferings with and for Christ as he proclaimed the Gospel in the Roman Empire (see e.g. 2 Cor. 4 - 6).

In his marvelous Letter to Rome, Paul made much use of the word "justification", a word closely tied to "righteousness" and "justice". He used it to explain what it means to be in a covenant relationship with God through believing the Gospel (see Rom.1:16-17; 3:21-31 & 5:1-2). It is to be placed by God Himself in a right relationship with God because of the merits of Jesus Christ through whom our sins are forgiven and the way to communion with God restored. It is to be declared righteous or just (in God's heavenly court) and to be placed in the way of becoming righteous and just. To be justified by faith is to be in God's covenant of grace and the recipient of His covenant mercy and faithfulness. It is to be able to know Him as God for He has placed believers in a right relationship with Himself. Previously in their sinfulness they were in a wrong or non-relationship but now by grace they are in the most intimately close relationship possible with Him for they are heirs and joint-heirs with Christ of the kingdom of God (Rom.8:17). In fact Paul makes it clear in his Letters that we only know God because

He first knew us (see 1 Cor.8:3; 13:12 & Gal.4:9). God entered into personal contact with sinful human beings through the Incarnate Son and by the Holy Spirit. Only on this basis of His knowing them can they know Him.

To be placed in the way of personal, practical righteousness, which is the inner life of the new covenant, means being united with Jesus Christ in faith and by the Holy Spirit. Thus in Romans 8 Paul describes the intimacy which God, the Father, establishes with His adopted children. He places in their hearts the Holy Spirit whom He names the Spirit of Christ. By His presence believers are enabled to cry out from the depths of their beings, "Abba" (the familiar name for father in the Jewish home). Further, they experience the Spirit Himself praying through them, uttering prayers they themselves could never compose. Their prayer and their life is a response to the heavenly Father's gracious, loving initiative and continuing faithfulness. The response becomes a life of maturity in faith, hope and love.

Taking the broad range of images used in the New Testament of the relationship of God to those who are united to the Lord Jesus Christ in faith, we may notice their personal nature by briefly mentioning four. God is the heavenly Father and believers are His adopted children, the brethren of Christ and joint-heirs with him of the Father's kingdom. Thus we pray, "Our Father." Further, God (or Jesus Christ as God-Man) is the Lord and King and believers are His subjects and servants, who live to render to Him humble service. Then God (or Jesus Christ) is the Shepherd and believers are His sheep. Jesus said, "I am the good shepherd and know my sheep...my sheep hear my voice and I know them" (John 10:14ff.).

God (or Jesus Christ as God-Man) is the Bridegroom who loves the Church and in response the Church is the Bride who likewise loves and obeys the Bridegroom. The last image points to a vital intimacy and it is interesting to observe that the Hebrew verb "to know" can and does refer sometimes in the Old Testament to the intimate act of sexual intercourse (e.g. 1 Sam 1:19, "Elkanah knew Hannah, his wife). Therefore the knowing of the Bridegroom (Jesus) by the Bride (the Church) points to deep spiritual union and communion within the souls of the faithful with Christ Himself and because with Him, with the Father.

God and Self

Archbishop Cranmer and those who assisted him in the composition of the first *Books of Common Prayer* in the sixteenth century were greatly influenced by the Letter to the Romans. Traces of its teaching can be found at many points, not least in the service of Holy Communion. Another theme which is found in Common Prayer is the ancient Christian wisdom that all Christian holiness is contained in two things - the knowledge of God and the knowledge of self. Often Augustine of Hippo, whose *Confessions* is a true classic and whose writings have always been prized by Anglicans, exclaimed, "Lord, that I may know thee and that I may know myself." To claim that this prayer is a summary of the Common Prayer tradition of piety and devotion would not be an excessive claim! I think it is generally true.

The knowledge of God elevates the Christian believer while knowledge of self keeps him humble. Knowing God is that ascent wherein the believer contemplates the divine perfections and glory while knowing self is that descent which makes him see his own nothingness and sinfulness. That knowledge of God which raises the believer up to God also simultaneously humbles him by the comparison of himself with God as He is revealed in Jesus. Further, genuine self-knowledge, though it humbles the believer, also lifts him up through the necessity of approaching God to find comfort, forgiveness and solace through Christ Jesus. The true elevation of man is inseparable from his true humiliation - which is made crystal clear in the Anglican Common Prayer Tradition. To elevate man without humbling him is to cause pride; and to humble him without exalting him is to bring misery without hope. Thus to complain as do some modern teachers of liturgy that the Common Prayer Tradition is preoccupied with concerns of guilt, sin and justification is to go against the wisdom of Scripture and tradition. Unless worshippers see their sin, guilt and hopelessness how can they see that in Jesus Christ alone is salvation?

To know self is as necessary for holiness as is the knowing of God. To know self is to treat the self justly for to know ourselves as we really are is to see ourselves as God Himself sees us. Consider the question, Who am I? I am nothing in and of myself for from all eternity I was not and there was no reason why I should exist or be what I am. My existence is the effect of God's will alone - not mine or anyone else's. Were God to withdraw His powerful, sustaining word and power my being would cease to be. All I am and can be comes from God and is dependent upon Him and thus there is nothing in myself to love. In fact since I have sinned against my Creator I justly deserve His punishment. I have offended and continue to offend the Lord my God. I have become His enemy and I transgress His law. I fail in essential duties to Him and my fellow creatures for in me the tendency to sin has become a fixed habit and a strong inclination. Further, I cannot help myself out of this mess. God Himself must lift me up if I am to be raised.

A significant statement is left out of the General Confession in Morning Prayer in Rite I of *BCP* (1979). On first sight the Confession from *BCP* (1928) and (1979) appear to be the same but the reality of original sin or the diseased, deceitful heart (Jer.17:9; Mark 7:18-23) is missing from the latter. "There is no health in us" is profoundly true and is wholly recognized by those, tutored by Holy Scripture, who see themselves as God sees and knows them.

Thus we learn from our Bibles and Prayer Books that to be genuine Christians we must recognize and admit that we are nothing of ourselves, that we receive all things from God, both in the order of nature and of grace; and, further, that we expect all things from Him in the order of glory in the age to come. As the Collect for the Fourth Sunday after Trinity puts it:

O God, the protector of all that trust in thee, without whom nothing is strong, nothing is holy; Increase and multiply upon us thy mercy; that, thou being our ruler and guide, we may so pass through things temporal, that we finally lose not the things eternal. Grant this, O heavenly Father, for the sake of Jesus Christ our Lord. Amen.

This knowing of God and self inspired by the Holy Spirit is in part intellectual but it also is a knowing by the heart. By this knowledge of God the whole soul is penetrated, reformed, renewed and ennobled so that it begins to want to know and to love what God Himself commands and loves. To know God is to possess a lively faith, a firm hope, an ardent love, a filial fear and reverence, a total trust in times of trial and testing, and an entire submission to His gracious and perfect will. This is the form of knowing taught and encouraged by the Common Prayer Tradition.

To know God is thus a knowing by the whole soul. It is to know God in and through the mind (to have right thoughts about Him and to contemplate Him through His self-unveiling in Revelation), in and through the heart (to direct one's affections to Him so as to trust Him and His Word, to delight in Him, love Him, rejoice in His grace and fear His holy name) and through the will (in the obedience of faith in daily life). Of course people are different— some are more intellectual than others, while some are more affective than others. For some the mind descends into the heart in knowing God while for others the heart rises to contain the mind in knowing God. There is of course place for both types of personalities and the Common Prayer Tradition is wide enough for all kinds of people who come to the knowledge of God in faith in different ways. What this tradition does not cater for is merely an affective knowing - that is, a religion only of feelings. Instruction in basic Christian doctrine and biblical teaching is fundamental to the Anglican Way and this intellectual understanding ought to be there even in people who are primarily affective or feeling persons.

His Majesty

One of the great losses in modern worship—and thus modern Christianity—is that of the inner sense of the glorious Majesty, the wonderful transcendence and greatness of the Lord our God. "The Lord reigneth, he is clothed with majesty" (Ps.93:1); "I will speak of the glorious honor of thy majesty" (Ps.145:5). This recognition of Majesty has been called "a sense of the numinous" and "the fear of the Lord." So often Anglicans have sung: "The LORD is a great God and a great King...O come let us worship and bow down" (Ps.95). In the Bible one of the most obvious examples of the recognition of Majesty is the abasement and attitude of Isaiah in the Temple when he saw the glorious majesty of God, the King above all kings, and heard the angelic cry of worship, "Holy, Holy Holy" (Is.6).

If this deep conviction and inner sense of the transcendent, awesome Mystery (*Mysterium Tremendum*) who is God, is absent, then the resulting low view of God, (which regrettably can occur and has even occurred where there is a general commitment to Trinitarian Theism) has not only been the cause of a general diminishing of a sense of awe and wonder in worship but also of a host of practical errors and evils within the churches. Apparently so few seem to be aware of this loss because any vital sense of divine transcendence is absent from the surrounding culture as well as from the popular religious mind of today.

Further, so much emphasis has been placed in popular piety on God as personal, that is, personal in the sense that we are personal - weak, ineffective and inadequate—that we have lost the sense of the omnipotent and almighty LORD who is our God. Certainly He is personal but personal as the

LORD, who is majestic and great and who in His sovereign freedom establishes personal relationships with His creatures.

Few Christians and even fewer preachers appear to have high and lofty thoughts of the LORD our God: instead of being lost in wonder, love and praise at the thought of His Majesty we tend to think of Him only as around us and with us here and now. Of course He is omnipresent in the created order by the Holy Spirit and thus immanent in this world; but, He is only immanent because He is first transcendent, high and lifted up as Isaiah saw and knew Him in his vision. Perhaps the problem is that we think from the immanence of God towards His transcendence rather than from His transcendence to His immanence. In fact, it is probably true to say that there is an emerging sense of the irrelevance of the older Christian doctrine of the transcendence of the Lord our God, for modern people appear to need a God with whom they can easily identify and be a part of or negotiate with.

If we could regain the conviction in mind and heart that it is only by the creating and sustaining dynamic word of the LORD that each of us and everything around us actually exists and is kept in being then we would realize that God, the Creator, must be transcendent to be immanent. And if to recognize that He is the transcendent Creator, the infinite, eternal Majesty on high, glorious in holiness and perfect in purity, wholly beyond our thoughts and aspirations, then we would also both begin to appreciate His mercy and grace in revealing Himself to us and His infinite condescension in becoming Man, bone of our bone and flesh of our flesh. To this end we could do nothing more useful than meditate upon Isaiah 40:12ff. where the greatness and majesty of God is so very powerfully presented—"To whom will ye compare me that I should be like him? says the Holy One" (verse 25).

We learn in the Book of Proverbs, that the fear of the Lord is not only the beginning of wisdom but also the beginning of knowledge. There can only be godly fear in the soul when there are large views of God and small views of man. Filial fear is not fear of being judged and cast into hell but it is the awe, reverence, humble dependence and profound sense of dependence of the child of God upon the holy Lord God of hosts. This godly fear is encouraged in the Common Prayer Tradition by the repeated addressing of God as "Almighty God" at the beginning of Collects (and happily it is generally preserved in the *BCP*, 1979).

The Lord our God is holy with an absolute, almighty holiness that knows no degrees and this He cannot impart to His creatures for He is God and they are the work of His creative power. Yet there is a relative and contingent holiness which the Lord shares with the holy angels in heaven and with believing sinners on earth. The will of God is the sanctification of mankind in Christ and His command in both the Old and New Testaments is, "Be ye holy for I am holy" (Lev. 11:44; 1 Pet.1:16). God shares His holiness with those who know Him through imputation of Christ's righteousness (in Justification) and impartation of the indwelling Holy Spirit (in Sanctification). The Common Prayer Tradition faithfully sets forth this sharing.

5

BAPTISM AND CONFIRMATION

Knowing God as His adopted child begins for the Christian at holy Baptism. In the case of adults there will have been a preliminary and preparatory knowing as they are drawn to Christ in what we may call an initial conversion and as they begin to prepare for full incorporation into Christ, crucified and risen, and membership of his Body, the Church. In the third and fourth centuries adults went through a long period of preparation in the catechetical schools before the final preparation in Lent leading to baptism on Easter Eve. In modern times we have made the preparation less exacting, but there are moves afoot to recover a longer and deeper preparation for entry into the full fellowship of the church. This preparation is so necessary today for the tentacles of secularist culture have entered our minds and hearts and corrupted them so deeply that we need a new view of the world and of God in order to develop Christian thinking, feeling and acting. One problem is—do we have the clergy and lay leadership to do this teaching?

With infants there is no obvious preliminary knowing of God and thus their knowing of God—or more strictly God's gracious knowing them as His adopted children—begins at Baptism and comes to fruition with Confirmation. At least this is how it ought to be but in this instance God's grace coming to fruition in their lives is in part dependent upon faithful nurturing and teaching of the baptized by parents and godparents (sponsors). Therefore the actual coming to know God in a personal way seems to occur more readily and easily when the baptized infant is surrounded by faithful prayer, godly example and sound teaching.

Originally what we call Baptism and Confirmation belonged together and were one, occurring in the one service and usually at Easter Eve in the early centuries of the Church. However, from the fifth century onwards, and with the great increase in the number of people professing Christianity, many more babies than adults were brought for Baptism and so the separation of Confirmation (really the last part of the rite of baptism) from Baptism developed in the West (but not in the East where the priest administered chrism [anointing with oil] as part of Baptism of infants). Thus in the West, from the Middle Ages to the modern day, the precise relation of Baptism and Confirmation has sometimes not been as clearly stated as it could have been: and this is reflected in the question whether or not baptized children ought to be brought to, or encouraged to, receive Holy Communion before their Confirmation—and in fact whether Confirmation is truly necessary.

Baptism

There is provision for both the baptism of adults and infants in the *BCP* (1928) and *BCP* (1962). The rite of holy Baptism has five parts to it: (1) the Preparation (which represents what has survived from the ancient catechetical ceremonies of the early Church); (2) the promises of the candidates or their sponsors/godparents taking on the duties of the covenant of grace; (3) the Blessing of the water in the Font; (4) the act of Baptism, and (5) a final Thanksgiving.

In the first part consisting of an exhortation, prayers and reading of the Gospel, the truth that it is God who calls and brings people into covenant with Him and thus into His Kingdom and Church is most clearly acknowledged. In fact this understanding is summarized in the prayer: *"Almighty and everlasting God, heavenly Father, we give thee humble thanks that thou hast vouchsafed to call us to the knowledge of thy grace and faith in thee: increase this knowledge and confirm this faith in us evermore. Give thy Holy Spirit to this child...etc."*

The promises made by the one to be baptized or the sponsors of the infant may be described as the response to the grace of God offered to mankind in Jesus Christ. They can only promise because God has come to them, called them and promised them the riches of His grace. It is of note that they say, "I will, by God's help," and that human promises are immediately followed by four supplications which, in addressing the God of all mercy for help, give expression to the mystical, spiritual and moral meaning of baptism. For example, the first supplication is :"O merciful God, grant that like as Christ died and rose again, so this child [or this thy servant] may die to sin and rise to newness of life."

The Blessing of the Font is an ancient practice since prayers for the sanctification of the water formed a part of the baptismal liturgy from earliest times. The physical water does not change its chemical composition through prayer but it is consecrated or set aside to be the outward and visible expression of an inward and spiritual cleansing. In fact it is related in its spiritual function to the water and blood which flowed from our Lord's pierced side (John 19:34). Once again therefore, we see that the initiative is with God; human beings are the recipients, not the initiators, of grace. All that they have is from God and by God in grace.

The formula of Baptism is taken from Matthew 28:19 and is a fully Trinitarian formula. To pronounce the threefold name of the One God over a person is to state and confess that he or she belongs to God and is His forever. The Name of God here stands for God Himself and thus we hallow the name of God. In other words, God is admitting this person into full membership and relationship of His covenant of grace. To sign him or her with the sign of the Cross makes clear that the covenant of grace is in, by and through Christ crucified: thus those who are in Christ are to take up their cross and follow Him and continue in His name the war against the world, the flesh and the devil, until he comes again in power and glory.

Finally, grateful hearts offer Thanksgiving for the union of the baptized with the Lord Jesus Christ, who was crucified and died but who is risen from the dead and reigns in glory. They have died to sin and are alive to God and must now put this divine truth into practical daily living with the help of the Holy Spirit. With infants the responsibility to make the presence of Christ effective in their lives devolves of course upon parents and sponsors.

There is a solemn duty laid upon the local church to pray for those who have been baptized as infants and await their Confirmation. A Collect provided in *BCP* (1928) for children encourages this constant prayer:

O Lord Jesus Christ, who dost embrace children with the arms of thy mercy, and dost make them living members of thy Church; give them grace, we pray thee, to stand fast in the faith, to obey thy word and to abide in thy love; that, being made strong by the Holy Spirit, they may resist temptation and overcome evil, and may rejoice in the life that now is, and dwell with thee in the life that is to come; through thy merits O merciful Saviour, who with the Father and the Holy Ghost livest and reignest one God, world without end. Amen.

To pray thus is to encourage the duty of bringing children up in "the nurture and admonition of the Lord."

The substance of the teaching to be given to baptized children before they are brought to Confirmation is given in the Catechism or Offices of Instruction. As the covenant partners of God they are to know what His law is (Ten Commandments) what their faith is (the Apostles' Creed) and how to pray (the Lord's Prayer). Further, they are to know what are the sacraments of the new covenant and who are the ministers of Christ in the Church. The Collects which are included in the Offices make it abundantly clear that it is only possible to please God through the assistance of His grace. For example:

O Almighty God, who alone canst order the unruly wills and affections of sinful men; grant unto thy people, that they may love the thing which thou commandest, and desire that which thou dost promise; that so, among the sundry and manifold changes of the world, our hearts may surely there be fixed, where true joys are to be found; through Jesus Christ our Lord. Amen.

Another Collect asks that the baptized may have "the spirit to think and do always such things as are right" for in and of ourselves we cannot do any good [good that is good before God himself].

I often think of a Latin expression used by Martin Luther. Each morning as he arose from his bed he would say aloud, *Baptizus sum* (I have been baptized or I am a baptized Christian). In saying this he was reminding himself of what it means to be baptized (and confirmed) and he was expressing his prayer that each day he would live as one who in Christ has died to sin and who in Christ is to be filled with the new, resurrection life of Christ, which is the life of the kingdom of God. There is a very intimate connection between the state of being baptized and the vocation to live a genuinely Christian life. Although all is of grace there is a real sense also in which all is of the baptized believer. This truth is wonderfully captured in the words,

I would not work my soul to save

For that my Lord has done.

But I would work like any slave,

For love of God's dear Son.

I believe we can learn and profit from what Luther said and practiced for we all are called to demonstrate in daily living the meaning of our baptism into Christ. And, as Confirmation makes clear, we can do so because—and only because—of the presence and power of the Holy Spirit, who indwells the souls of the baptized.

Confirmation

There has been much discussion and dispute in recent times within the Anglican Communion on the nature and purpose of Confirmation. Is it a sacrament in its own right or is it the completion of Holy Baptism? And if in the case of infants it is only the completion of Baptism is it really necessary? Should baptized children who are not confirmed be admitted to Holy Communion?

It seems to me that Confirmation is the conclusion of the sacrament of Holy Baptism. It may be called a sacrament in the sense that it is the final part of the rite of Baptism which has been held back until such time as the child truly understands and appreciates what is the content of the covenantal obligation to God that already by grace he or she stands in. Thus as long as the Church advocates and practices infant baptism so long ought she to take Confirmation seriously. And First Communion should normally follow Confirmation.

Confirmation is necessary in terms of providing the opportunity for the fulfilling of the human side of the covenant of grace (i.e. public commitment to Jesus Christ as Lord) and it is most useful as the opportunity to provide the reason for sound, preparatory instruction to those who are now seriously taking on the duties of the baptismal covenant (already promised by their sponsors). Here preparation for Confirmation functions in much the same way as did preparation for Baptism in the Early Church and as catechetical teaching functions in missionary situations today.

Where the local church is truly concerned for the spiritual and moral welfare of those to be confirmed she prays for them. A Collect is actually provided in *BCP* (1928) for this obligation:

O God, who through the teaching of thy Son Jesus Christ didst prepare the disciples for the coming of the Comforter; make ready, we beseech thee, the hearts and minds of thy servants who at this time are seeking to be strengthened by the gift of the Holy Spirit through the laying on of hands, that, drawing near with penitent and faithful hearts, they may evermore be filled with the power of his divine indwelling; through the same Jesus Christ our Lord. Amen.

The making ready is both a work of God and a work of man. God does His work invisibly through the ministry of the Holy Spirit but the local church does her work through wise teaching and fervent praying for the confirmands.

Now to the service itself, which is simple and brief. Those to be confirmed are presented to the bishop, who asks them whether they are ready to renew the solemn promises and vows made by or for them at holy Baptism. They are to ratify and confirm these and in response they say, "I do". Then he asks them:"Do ye promise to follow Jesus Christ as your Lord and Saviour?" (which faith and following, we may note, is surely the very heart of the Christian religion and the essence of what it is to know God).

Following responsive versicles from the Psalter, there is an ancient prayer, offered by the bishop for those about to be confirmed. It is informed by Isaiah 11:2 (not from the Latin or Hebrew but from the Greek translation known as the Septuagint) where the seven (rather than six) gifts of the Holy Spirit are found. These are the spirit of wisdom and understanding, the spirit of counsel and ghostly strength, the spirit of knowledge and true godliness, and holy fear.

Commenting on the sevenfold gifts the late A.J.Mason made the following observations which I find helpful:

None of the gifts are directly of moral virtue. They are gifts which set a man in a position to acquire moral virtues, and incline him to practice them; but they do not in any way supply him with virtues ready-made, or relieve their possessor from the necessity of carefully forming right habits of action and feeling. It seems that all the sanctifying work of the Holy Ghost is done by an inward teaching, which commends to us the true principles of moral choice, and an inward strengthening, by which the forces of Christ are imparted to us, that we may act, and act perseveringly, upon the convictions which the Holy Ghost has wrought in us. (*The Relation of Confirmation to Baptism*, 1891, p.481.)

I would add that this is entirely what the New Testament leads us to expect and think, for the indwelling Spirit (whose work Paul so lovingly describes in Romans 8 and elsewhere) prompts, guides and inspires us so that we may be and do what is pleasing to God. Only in this way of being treated as persons can we know God personally.

Though there is no required anointing with oil (chrism), the Bishop does lay his hands upon each person and call upon the Lord to defend and empower His child (through humble reliance upon the Holy Spirit's presence and power) to live faithfully and come unto His everlasting kingdom. And following the Lord's Prayer there are two prayers before the Blessing. In the first, the bishop prays thus:

Let thy fatherly hand, we beseech thee, ever be over them; let thy Holy Spirit ever be with them; and so lead them in the knowledge and obedience of thy Word, that in the end they may obtain everlasting life...

Like other confirmed Christians the newly confirmed are to walk under the protection of God and in the power of His Spirit as they prayerfully meditate upon, and thereby are prepared for obedience to, the written Word of God. Knowledge of the Word is the route into the knowing of God as God. And, as we shall see, this knowledge is increased through the Daily Offices of Morning and Evening Prayer (for which see chapter six) and is enhanced and made personal in Holy Communion (for which see chapter eight).

6

MORNING AND EVENING PRAYER

For Christians the obligation and tradition of daily prayer is traced not only to the Jewish discipline adopted and developed by the early Church but to Jesus Himself. As a boy he was taught the Jewish custom of praying three times a day. The morning prayer consisted of the meditative recital of the *Shema* (Deut. 6:4-7) which confesses the Oneness of the Lord and the duty to love Him, and the *Tephilla*, a prayer made up of eighteen acts of blessing God (benedictions)— e.g. "Blessed art thou, O Lord, God of Abraham..." The afternoon prayer required only the Tephilla while the evening prayer was the same as morning prayer. Of course the use of the Shema and Tephilla was only the basic structure and around it and with it the pious Jew prayed the Psalter and offered his own petitions. Jesus obviously used it and in using it made it the means of communion with His Father in heaven, for at the age of twelve He told His mother, "I must be about my Father's business" (Luke 2:49).

The services of Morning and Evening Prayer, sometimes called Matins and Evensong and referred to as the Daily Offices, the Choir Offices and the Divine Office, are directly descended from the system of daily services or Canonical Hours of the medieval Church. These developed from the simple morning and evening prayer of the early Church and are to be found in the Breviaries used by the monastic and secular clergy.

It is generally recognized that the creation of Morning and Evening Prayer in the sixteenth century was an important advance in engaging the laity in the duty and joy of daily worship and prayer. The late Massey H Shepherd Jr. put it well when he wrote:

It was the genius of the great Reformers, such as Luther and Cranmer, to see the potential advantage to the Church of making the Daily Offices a means of corporate worship for all the faithful, the laity as well as the clergy, and, in particular, a vehicle for the recovery of a knowledge of the Holy Scriptures by all the people of God. To achieve these ends required not only the translation of the offices into the vernacular, but a very practical simplification and reduction in both the number of these offices and their content. The artistry of Cranmer's accomplishment of these purposes has been the admiration of all succeeding generations. (*The Oxford American Prayer Book Commentary*, 1950, introduction, p.l.)

We certainly admire the literary artistry but we are also grateful to God that the daily services can and were intended to be, under the blessing of God, a wonderful vehicle for the knowledge of God through the encounter with Him through His Word and in prayer.

In *Prayer Book Studies VI* published in 1957 the Standing Liturgical Commission stated:

The genius of our Common Prayer is in no instance more clearly exemplified than in the Daily Offices of Morning and Evening Prayer. Out of the elaborate, complicated Canonical Hours of the medieval Breviary the sixteenth century Reformers produced a pattern of daily praise and prayer that was loyal to tradition, solidly Scriptural in content, simple and convenient in execution, balanced and artful in design. The older Latin Offices had been a primary duty of the clergy, the monks and friars, upon whom their recitation was imposed by canonical law. But the Reformers intended their simpler, vernacular forms to be a means of corporate worship and edification in the knowledge of God's Word for all the laity no less than the clergy. In this purpose their labors have borne abundant fruit. To no other part of the Prayer Book have the lay people shown greater attachment and responsiveness.

These are fine words and it is interesting to note that after Vatican II the Roman Catholic Church caught up with Cranmer! I refer to the provisions in the document, *General Instruction on the Liturgy of the Hours (1971)*.

It is perhaps impractical to expect all faithful Anglicans to go twice daily to their parish church in order to say the Daily Office. However, there is no reason why either or both of the services should not be used in the home as the basis for personal and/or family prayers. Alternatively church members who live near each other can gather in homes on a regular basis to pray one or both of these offices. Where there is a desire and a will to pray them a way will be found.

The logic of the services

The daily services are for the covenant people of God, for those who walk by faith in faithfulness - or at least desire so to do. Thus Morning Prayer and Evening Prayer begin with a call from God through his minister to his people to engage in penitence, praise and thanksgiving, instruction from God through His Word and petitionary prayer. This call is achieved through the recital of sentences from Scripture and an Exhortation, which fully recognizes the sinfulness of the human condition before God.

Having been summoned and having come before Almighty God as believers or people of faith, the covenant people of God must confess their sins, recognizing that in and of themselves they have nothing good to offer unto their gracious, faithful, covenant Lord who is the God of all mercy. So kneeling down and thereby submitting to the sovereign mercy of God, His people confess not only their rebellion against Him ("we have offended against thy holy laws") but the actual sinfulness of their souls ("There is no health in us").

The Declaration of divine absolution and remission of sins pronounced by the priest or bishop is composed of a medley of scriptural sentences. To all who repent of their sins and believe the promises of the Gospel there is full and free forgiveness as there is also a call to "be pure and holy."

The rest of the service may be described as an expression of responsive faith. The faith which has responded to God's call and heard His promise of forgiveness and eternal life now speaks to God and hears from Him. It is entirely fitting and appropriate therefore that believers begin their response by saying the prayer composed by our Lord Himself—the Lord's Prayer, which is the model for all prayer and the summary of all prayer. And following this the heart, now warmed by God's gracious presence and word, is ready to praise His name. This is done through the versicles taken from Psalm 51:15 which lead into the *Gloria Patri* or the "little doxology" - "Glory to the Father and to the Son and to the Holy Spirit..." Christian souls are now ascending in and with Christ to heaven to bow before and adore the One God, who is a Trinity of Persons. They not only affirm trinitarian theism but they worship this LORD God.

Responsive faith continues to praise the Lord through the *Venite* (Ps 95) which celebrates the Majesty of God, the Creator, Sustainer, Provider and Judge. Then follows the meditative reading or chanting of the appointed psalms. These are prayed in, with and through Jesus Christ, and not merely as prayers from the Old Testament (see below chapter seven for a full treatment of the Psalter). This contemplative, reflective hearing is continued with the listening to what God has to say and teach from the first lesson, read from the Old Testament. It is heard not merely as a reading but as a lesson (i.e. a teaching from God Himself through the illumination of the Holy Spirit on the mind).

Having heard the Word of God read, the people of faith join again in the worship and praise of Almighty God. This is achieved through the use of the *Te Deum laudamus* (the magnificent hymn of praise to the Father, the Son and the Holy Spirit) or the shorter *Benedictus es, Domine* (from the addition to the Book of Daniel in the Apocrypha) or the longer *Benedicite, omnia opera Domini* (from the same source as the *Benedictus*).

God has yet more to say unto His believing people and so there is read the Second Lesson, this time from the New Testament, to be heard with obedient, reflective faith. Following it, there is again a wholly appropriate song with which to join in the praise of God. This is achieved through the recital of either the *Benedictus* (the Song of Zechariah, father of John the Baptist) or Psalm 100, the *Jubilate Deo*.

Now praising, believing souls are ready to speak to God and tell Him what they believe as baptized Christians on the basis of His Revelation to them through sacred Scripture. Thus they join in the Apostles' Creed, each one making his or her personal profession of faith, "I believe." On some occasions they may use the longer and more theologically developed confession of faith, the Nicene Creed. The Creed is a word addressed to God, a word shared with fellow Christians and a concise word of hope and good news offered to the world.

Finally, forgiven, praising and believing souls express their faith and commitment to Jesus as Lord by engaging in petitionary and intercessory prayers for themselves and others, especially those with heavy responsibilities in State and Church. Believers pray for others in the confidence that the Lord God who has blessed them will also bless those for whom they pray. They pray in the name of the Lord Jesus to the Father in heaven, in the power of the Holy Spirit. The set prayers, which are all memorable in style and theology, include the two great prayers which all Anglicans ought to know by heart—the Prayer for all Conditions of Men and the General Thanksgiving. The final prayer of the service is the Grace, taken straight from the Bible (from 2 Cor.13:14).

Such is the logic of faith of Morning Prayer - and the same logic is there in Evening Prayer. Modern usage often begins the Office at the Versicles and thereby destroys the logic of faith which requires us to begin where we are, in our sin, in order to rise by and in Christ as forgiven people to the praise of God Almighty. This is why in the Common Prayer Tradition the confession of sin is not optional. Such is the human condition, even of the best of us, that we always need to confess our sins of commission and omission, and to recognize both the bias to sin which is deep in our souls and our participation in the sins of mankind as a whole.

One important dimension of the Daily Office often mentioned by the saints is that it is the voice of the bride addressing her Bridegroom and it is the very prayer which Christ Himself, in and through His Body, addresses to the Father. Thus by offering praise to God the Church on earth joins in the heavenly litany and canticles of praise of the angels and archangels. Earth and heaven combine in the heavenly liturgy.

Intimately connected on earth to the Daily Office is the Litany or General Supplication. It is to be used after the Third Collect of Morning or Evening Prayer. The Litany is composed of (a) solemn addresses to the Holy Trinity; (b) petitions for deliverance from evil; (c) entreaties addressed to the Lord Jesus recalling His saving deeds for us; (d) petitions and intercessions ending with the "O Lamb of God...", the "Lord have mercy" and the Lord's Prayer, and (e) a final supplication, composed of responsive versicles and collects. The entire Litany, apart from the beginning and the ending is addressed to the Lord Jesus.

The aim of all prayer is to know God and thus the Litany ends with this prayer:

We humbly beseech thee, O Father, mercifully to look upon our infirmities; and for the glory of thy Name, turn

*from us all those evils that we most justly have deserved;
and grant, that in all our troubles we may put our whole
trust and confidence in thy mercy, and evermore trust
thee in holiness and pureness of living, to thy honour
and glory; through our only Mediator and Advocate,
Jesus Christ our Lord. Amen.*

To know God is to live in utter dependence upon His
mercy and strength.

Meditative participation

Faith hears and reads Scripture as the Word of God.
Therefore it hears prayerfully and meditatively. This spirit
is captured in Psalm 19, "Let the words of my mouth and
the meditation of my heart, be acceptable in thy sight, O
LORD, my strength and my redeemer" (verse 14). It is stated
with clarity in the Collect for the Second Sunday in Advent:

*Blessed Lord, who hast caused all holy Scriptures to be
written for our learning; grant that we may in such wise
hear them, mark, learn, and inwardly digest them, that
by patience and comfort of thy holy Word, we may
embrace and ever hold fast, the blessed hope of
everlasting life, which thou has given us in our Saviour
Jesus Christ. Amen.*

This Collect assumes what the Church of God has
always believed—that the Holy Bible is the record, inspired
by the Holy Spirit, of God's self-revelation to human beings.
Further, it assumes that it was written under God's superin-
tendence for our benefit, that we may learn therein by the
illumination of our minds by the Holy Spirit of the nature of
God and of His salvation offered to us in Jesus, the Christ.
To hear or read Scripture prayerfully and in faith is to place
oneself in the position to be taught by God, where the
Lessons become truly teaching sessions of the Holy Spirit.

In the Collect we pray that we may hear the Lessons
(that is hear not only with our physical ears but with the
spiritual ears of our soul and thus allow the Word of God to

enter our minds and hearts and wills); that we may mark them (that is notice the particular message or teaching, doctrinal, moral or spiritual which God is giving us through the Lesson); that we may learn (that is take to heart to be obeyed and learn off by heart in order to meditate upon later, where appropriate); and that we may inwardly digest them (that is allow the teaching of the Word of God to become food for our souls through our inward receiving of its contents in the mind, with the affections and by the will). By such receiving of the Word of God we gain knowledge about and grow in the knowing of the living God and thus embrace and hold fast "the blessed hope of everlasting life" through Jesus Christ.

Some may raise the problem of the agnostic assumptions of modern Biblical Studies and claim that they make such meditative, prayerful reading of Scripture to be impossible today. I do not think that truly modern, scientific study of Holy Scripture in any way puts a barrier in the way of meditative reading. However, I can see that a small dose of it can have this effect; regrettably too many people today get a small dose of it from second-best practitioners and make their judgments on inferior knowledge and understanding. I have every confidence that the Word of God can and does speak to us as clearly and effectually today as it did when the Prayer Book was first written in 1549-1552.

In my book, *Meditating as a Christian* (Harper-Collins, 1991) I made a distinction between informative reading and formative reading, as a way to state the nature of biblical meditation which is possible in the Daily Office (or, of course, at other times as well). Most of the reading we do is to gain information—from newspaper, book, letter, report, journal and magazine. The information may be for work or leisure or for another purpose. Now to read the Bible for information, that is informatively, is to study it as a historical, religious book. Biblical Studies are usually sophisticated forms of informative reading. The reader is here in charge and looks at the Book as an object which he or she is examining.

In contrast, formative reading is to read in such a way as to be formed by what is read. It is to read slowly, preferably aloud, so that the Word can be seen, heard and tasted. It is also to read prayerfully and expectantly. In this approach the intention is to put Jesus Christ in charge so that He can speak to the reader and hearer through the Word and by the Spirit. To read and hear in this way in the Daily Office is an art to be cultivated and cannot be achieved overnight. To develop the art may require returning to the Lessons at the end of the Office and re-reading them in the formative mode. Or it may require preparing for their reading in the Office by looking at them or studying them in advance. At first it may only be possible to treat one of the Lessons seriously. We must begin where we are and grow in grace and in the knowledge of God for God is a tender Father who leads us on by His gracious hand.

Repetition

One of the aims of modern Liturgy appears to be to keep people from staying with one form of worship, one set of texts and prayers. However, there is great spiritual benefit in the use of the same texts day by day, especially if they are, as in the Daily Office, excellent Canticles and Prayers in fine, memorable English. However this benefit only applies if they are said, sung or prayed in faith with the mind in the heart. They will become utterly boring if they are merely repeated because that is what is required. To the heart which is seeking to know and love God they become the very words through which that knowledge and faith is expressed. Familiarity with them increases their usefulness as the content of the human response to God's gracious invitation to draw near to Him and behold His glory.

If they are learned off by heart then each day as they are prayed the mind is able both to see and to pour into them ever deeper meaning, the affections are able to be raised in delight, peace and love towards God, while the will is moved in resolve to obey God at all times. Further, the stability of the structure of fixed Canticles and Prayers provides the appropriate context for the changing Psalms and Lessons. The latter can be appreciated and their content spiritually received because of the devotional and theological reliability of the structure in which they are placed.

In fact the logic of faith, which we have noticed informing Daily Prayer is the logic of the whole of Common Prayer. We are summoned by God to daily prayer to hear His Word, utter His praise, offer prayers and supplications and be strengthened for our vocation in daily life. We are further summoned to the Lord's Table each Sunday, the first day of the week and the day of the Resurrection of the Lord in order to meet Him in Word and Sacrament - in the most spiritually intimate communion as we hear again His Word and receive His Body and Blood.

The lectionary of weekdays and of Sunday is also harmonized by this logic of faith. The lectionary is an ordered program of readings from Scripture for the public worship of the Church. The Common Prayer Tradition presents in the lectionary readings both for Sundays (and the week after) and Holy Days, and also for the Sunday and week-day offices of Morning and Evening Prayer. The interrelation and inter-dependence of these programs of readings, together with the comprehensive doctrinal unity which they create, is the fruit of a long development. Guiding this development has been the principle of Holy Scripture understood as a doctrinal instrument of salvation (which means that Holy Scripture has a content, that this content is thinkable and that its intelligible content is doctrine). All this is to say that by such an arrangement the Church consciously puts herself under the rule and authority of Scripture.

Perhaps a final comment is needed on the singing of hymns. Where they are used they ought to become a part of the logic of faith and not disturb or stand in opposition to that logic. Not all hymns are suitable and some are suitable only at specific points in worship.

Advice from William Beveridge

[Writing nearly three hundred years ago William Beveridge, Bishop of St Asaph in Wales, gave some first-class advice on how to prepare for and participate in corporate worship. This is what he wrote in his *The Great Necessity and Advantage of Public Prayer,* 1708.]

Here then is the great task we have to do in all our public devotions, even to keep our spirits or hearts in a right posture all the while that we are before God, who sees them, and takes special notice of their motions...Blessed be God, by His assistance we may do it, if we will but set ourselves in good earnest about it, and observe these few rules...

First, when you go to the house of God at the hour of prayer, be sure to leave all worldly cares and business behind you, entertaining yourselves, as ye go along, with these, or such like sentences of Scripture: *Like as the hart desireth the waterbrooks, so longeth my soul after thee, O God; my soul is athirst for God, yea, even the living God. When shall I come to appear before the presence of God?* (Ps. 42:1, 2). *O how amiable are thy dwellings, thou Lord of hosts! My soul hath a desire and longing to enter into the courts of the Lord. My heart and my flesh rejoice in the living God.* (Ps. 84:1, 2). *We will go into His tabernacle and fall low on our knees before His footstool.* (Ps. 132:7).

When ye come into the church say with Jacob, *How dreadful is this place! This is none other but the house of God; and this is the gate of heaven* (Gen. 28:17), or something to that purpose. And as soon as ye can get an opportunity, prostrate yourselves upon your knees before the Master of the house, the great God of heaven, humbly beseeching Him to unite your hearts unto Himself, to cleanse your thoughts by the inspiration of His Holy Spirit, to open your eyes, and to manifest Himself unto you, and to assist you with such a measure of grace in offering up these *spiritual sacrifices*, that they may be *acceptable* to Him by Jesus Christ.

And now set yourselves, in good earnest; as in God's sight, keeping your eye only upon Him, looking upon Him as observing what you think, as well as what you say or do, all the while you are before him.

While one or more of the *Sentences* out of God's Holy Word (wherewith we very properly begin our Devotions to Him) are *reading*, apprehend it as spoken by God Himself at first, and now repeated in your ears, to put you in mind of something, which He would have you to believe or do upon this occasion.

While the *Exhortation* is reading, hearken diligently to it, and take particular notice of every word and expression in it, as contrived on purpose to prepare you for the service of God, by possessing your minds with a due sense of His special presence with you, and of the great ends of your coming before Him at this time.

While you are confessing your sins with your mouth, be sure to do it also in your hearts, calling to mind every one, as many as he can, of those particular sins which he hath committed, either by doing what he ought not to do, or not doing what he ought, so as to repent sincerely of them, and steadfastly resolve never to commit them any more.

While the minister is pronouncing the *Absolution* in the name of God, every one should lay hold upon it for himself, so as firmly to believe, that upon true repentance, and faith in Christ, he is now discharged and absolved from all his sins, as certainly as if God Himself had declared it with His own mouth, as He hath often done it before, and now, by His ministers.

While you, together with the minister, are repeating the *Psalms* or *Hymns*, to the honour and glory of God, observe the minister's part as well as your own; and lift up your hearts, together with your voices, to the highest pitch you can, in acknowledging, magnifying and praising the infinite wisdom, and power, and goodness, and glory of the most high God in all His works, the wonders that He hath done, and still doth, for the children of men, and for you among the rest.

While God's *Word* is read in either of the chapters, whether of the *Old* or *New Testament* receive it not as the word of men but (as it is in truth) the Word of God, which effectually worketh in you that believe (1 Thess. 2:13). And therefore *hearken* to it with the same attention, reverence and faith, as you would have done, if you had stood by Mount Sinai, when God proclaimed the Law, and by our Saviour's side, when He published the Gospel.

While the *Prayers* or *Collects* are reading, although you ought not to repeat them aloud, to the disturbance of other people; yet you must repeat them in your hearts, your minds accompanying the minister from one prayer to another, and from one part of each prayer to the other, all along with affection suitable to the matter sounding in your ears, humbly adoring God according to the names, properties or works, which are attributed to Him at the beginning of each *Prayer*, earnestly desiring the good things which are asked Him in the body of it, for yourselves or others. And steadastly believing in Jesus Christ for His granting of them, when He is named, as He is at the end of each prayer, except that of *St Chrysostom*; because that is directed immediately to Christ Himself as promising, that *when two or three are gathered together in His name, He will grant their requests*, which is therefore very properly put at the end of all our daily prayers, and also the *Litany* (most part whereof is directed also to our Saviour) that when we have made all our *common supplications* unto Him, we may act our faith in Him again for God's granting of them according to His said promise. And so we may be dismissed with, *The Grace of our Lord Jesus Christ, the Love of God the Father, and the Communion or Fellowship of the Holy Ghost*; under which are comprehended all the blessings, that we can have, or can desire, to make us completely happy, both now and forever.

After the *Blessing*, it may be expedient still to continue for some time upon your knees, humbly beseeching Almighty God to pardon what He hath seen amiss in you, since you came into His presence; and that He would be graciously pleased to hear the prayers, and to accept of the praises, which you have offered up unto Him, through the merits of Jesus Christ our only Mediator and Advocate.

7

PRAYING THE PSALTER

Certainly the Psalter is at the very heart of the Daily Office. It is the inspired collection of prayers which the Church prays with and in Christ and which the individual Christian prays as a member of the Church, the Body of Christ. Today it is not easy for Christians who have had little or no instruction in liturgical prayer and who have not been taught how the Church over the centuries has used the Psalms to pray them as Christians. Certainly it is difficult to pray them in this manner if the only encounter with them is as a Gradual (appointed psalm verses to be sung or read between eucharistic readings) ; modern Episcopalians seem only to encounter the Psalter through the ten or so verses from one psalm between the Old Testament and New Testament readings in the modern Eucharist. Further (and I shall look at this in chapter eleven below) it is nearly impossible to pray the Psalms as a Christian from the inclusivist translations which are in the recent Canadian and American Prayer Books.

We need to bear in mind that we do not use the Psalter as if it were only an ancient Jewish book of prayers which were said or sung in the Temple, synagogue and home. Of course there is a legitimate, and for us today, necessary academic study which attempts to analyze the Psalter and to determine the original use and meaning of each of the Psalms in the worship and religious experience of Israel. In particular there has been valuable work on establishing the nature of the Hebrew poetry which uses a variety of parallel arrangements of lines of poetry as well as in associating particular psalms with specific festivals in Israel. Such study is what Old Testament scholars engage in and seminarians learn. The fruit of some of this study can be and has been assimilated and used profitably within the Church to aid her Liturgy and the prayers of her members. It belongs to what I called the informative reading of the Bible: yet it is scholarly, sophisticated, informative reading.

However, Christians have consistently used the Psalter formatively, following the way in which the Jews themselves used it before and in the time of Jesus. In Hebrew the Psalms are called *Tehillim*, "songs of praise"; in Greek they are called *Psalmoi*, "songs to be sung to the sound of the harp". Since they are inspired by God they have a timeless quality. In praying the psalms devout Jews thought of the psalms as prayers which are always relevant and always contemporary. They were and are always the prayer of Israel, or of the individual Israelite. They saw in the Psalter in its inspired verse not only their praises and thanksgivings, laments and complaints, petitions and intercessions, hopes and joys but also their prayer for the Messiah, the Deliverer of Israel. The Psalter was God's provision of prayer for His people to use in temple, synagogue and home. Since it had been inspired by His Spirit the LORD was committed by His gracious covenant relationship with Israel to hear those who prayed in its spirit and words.

Jesus, the Jew, entered into this tradition of daily praying the "songs of praise" which the Spirit of the Lord had inspired king David and others to compose. He saw His vocation in the first psalm - "Blessed is the man... whose delight is in the law of the LORD and in His law doth he meditate day and night." In the portraits and prophecies of the Messiah (e.g. Psalms 2, 72 & 110) Jesus saw His Messianic role as the anointed suffering King of Israel. We may claim that the Psalter was the Prayer Book of Jesus for the whole of His life: He quoted it in his public ministry and from it He prayed as He died on the Cross ("My God, my God, why hast thou forsaken me?", Psalm 22). He expired with a part of Psalm 31 on His lips: "Into thy hands I commend my spirit." Then, as the resurrected Lord, He met

His disciples and explained to them what was written concerning Him not only in the Law and the Prophets but also in the Psalms (Luke 24:44).

Against this background it was entirely to be expected that the first Christians would also use the Psalter and imitate their Lord's praying of it. They wanted to pray in the words inspired by the Holy Spirit as God's covenant people had long done . Thus we find that in the early Church the Psalms were prayed (said or sung) as the prayers of the new Israel whose Messiah and Lord is Jesus of Nazareth, the exalted King. Nearly fifty Psalms are cited in the New Testament and there they are invested with a Christian interpretation. This tradition of use and meaning is to be seen not only in the place of the Psalter in the emerging Liturgy of the Church but in the commentaries on the Psalter by such well-known bishops as Augustine of Hippo, Chrysostom, Hilary and Ambrose, not to mention Jerome to whom we owe the Latin Vulgate.

In the Introduction to the Divine Office of the Roman Catholic Church we receive this advice:

Whoever says the psalms in the name of the Church should pay attention to the full meaning of the Psalms, especially that messianic understanding which led the Church to adopt the Psalter. The messianic meaning is made completely manifest in the New Testament; it is in fact declared by Christ our Lord... Following this path, the Fathers took the whole Psalter and explained it as a prophecy about Christ and his Church; and for this same reason psalms were chosen for the sacred liturgy. Even if certain artificial interpretations were sometimes accepted, generally both the Fathers and the liturgy rightly heard in the psalms Christ calling out to his Father, or the Father speaking to the Son; they even recognized in them the voice of the Church, the apostles and martyrs...This christological interpretation in no way refers only to those psalms which are considered messianic but also extends to many in which without doubt there are mere appropriations. Such appropriations, however, have been commended by the tradition of the Church.

In the worship of the Church the Christian interpretation and use of the Psalter has been made clear through the use three aids: namely, the headings before each psalm, antiphons (a phrase or line which indicates the theme) and psalm collects (which summarizes the Christian meaning for the worshippers).

To pray the Psalter in this way is exceedingly difficult for those who have only known and examined the Psalter through modern academic study. It seems such an irrational move to the modern, secular mind to move from considering the Psalter only as the holy book and religious poetry of a pre-modern, near-eastern patriarchal society to praying its contents in a wholly spiritual and Christ-centred manner in a modern setting. Yet the logic of faith (which confesses the centrality and Lordship of Jesus) calls us to do just this and it can make this call because the Psalter was written under the inspiration of the Holy Spirit: thus God knew the greater purpose to which He would put it even though king David and other writers could not see into the long-term plan of God.

Certainly in the 150 Psalms are mirrored the ideals of religious piety and communion with God, of sorrow for sin and the search for perfection, of walking unafraid in darkness by the lamp of faith: of obedience to the law of God, delight in the worship of God, fellowship with the friends of God, reverence for the word of God; of humility under the chastening rod, trust when evil triumphs and wickedness prospers, serenity in the midst of storm. It is not surprising that the psalms of praise and lament can so easily become the prayer of honest, believing people today—be that prayer for themselves or for others. The Psalms inform our minds, warm our hearts and direct our wills towards the knowledge of God. Yet, without denying this use of the Psalter, the logic of faith calls upon Christians to know a deeper level of experience—to pray each Psalm with, in and through Christ.

Used in this Christian way the Psalms have advantages which no fresh compositions, however finely executed, can possibly have. Apart from their incomparable fitness to express our deep religious convictions and feelings, they are at the same time memorials of, and appeals to, former mercies and deliverances from God; they are acknowledgements of prophecies fulfilled; they point out the connection between the old and new dispensations (or administrations of God's covenant) and thereby teach us to admire and adore the wisdom of God displayed in both; further they provide us as we sing or say them with an inexhaustible variety of the noblest matter that can engage the meditations and contemplations of man.

Psalter (1928)

What praying the Psalms with and in Jesus actually means we shall examine below. Here it is perhaps necessary to make a comment on the actual Psalter printed in *BCP* (1928). Its origin goes back as far as 1536 and it was made by Miles Coverdale from the Latin Vulgate Psalter, originally translated into Latin from Hebrew by the great scholar, Jerome, in the fifth century. Thus we may note that the Latin reflected both a translation of the original and an usage in the Church which was then praying the Psalter in a Christ-centered way. The English translation captured this special character of the Vulgate and in doing so it served not primarily as an ancient Jewish text but as the thoroughly naturalized Prayer Book of Christians.

It is possible to find modern translations of the Psalms which are superior to the Coverdale version in terms of technical accuracy (e.g. the *Revised Standard Version* and the *New English Bible* - but not their successors the *NRSV* and the *REB* for they contain the ideology of inclusivism); and it is also possible to find versions which communicate the power and beauty of the Hebrew poetry (e.g. the Grail version). Yet for Christian use, in order that the *Gloria* may truly be said in reverence and truthfulness at the end of each Psalm, we need a version which captures the authentic Christ-centered nature of this Jewish and Christian Prayer Book. Happily the 1928 Psalter can still do this for us: in contrast, the 1979 Psalter is ill suited for this holy purpose.

Before we move on to look at the theme of Christ in the Psalms it may be useful to recall how the Psalms were viewed by Anglican leaders of the last century. Here is what John Henry Hobart, Bishop of New York, wrote in his much-used, *A Companion to the BCP* (1805). He wrote of the Coverdale Psalter as being a "more smooth and flowing" translation for church use than the Psalter in the *KJV*. Then he wrote:

> The Psalms were originally used in the service of the Jewish Temple and have been thence transferred into the Christian Church. These divinely inspired compositions breathe the sentiments of penitence, of prayer, and of praise, in strains most tender and sublime. By beautiful and interesting comparisons drawn from the works of nature and the customs of society, but principally by personal and ceremonial types and shadows, they display the excellence of Christian doctrine: the character, the offices, and the conditions of the Savior, and the circumstances of his Church and its members. As the Psalms therefore have a spiritual application and meaning, and are thus frequently applied by Christ and his apostles, it is no objection to the use of them that they contain sentiments and expressions applicable to the Jewish dispensation and to the particular circumstances of the king of Israel.

And he continued:

> Whatever the Psalmist says of the excellences of the law; of the ark, the temple, and the holy city of

Jerusalem, of the sacrifices on the Jewish altar; and of his own distresses, his temporal enemies and signal deliverances, may be easily applied to the Gospel, which is the law fulfilled; to the Christian Church, which the ark, the temple and Jerusalem prefigured; to that one great sacrifice of Christ still commemorated in the holy Eucharist, from which the Jewish sacrifices derived all their efficacy; and to the humiliation of the Savior to the enemies of his Church and people, and to the victories by which he wrought their redemption; all which were set forth in the humiliation, the enemies, and the victories of the frequently distressed and persecuted, yet finally triumphant, king of Israel.

Bishop Hobart then proceeded to explain how Christians may use the "bitter imprecations of David against his enemies" when they are prayed with, in and through Christ. For Anglicans who wanted to know more of the principles which govern the Christian use and praying of the Psalms he commended the Preface of Bishop George Horne's *Commentary on the Psalms*. Horne was Bishop of Norwich in England and his Commentary was much used in the early nineteenth century. We quote from it at the end of this chapter because, though historical study of the Psalms has continued, the Christian principles which guide the praying of the Psalms remain constant - simply because Jesus Christ is the same yesterday, today and forever (Heb.13:8).

Christ in the Psalms

In order to begin to appreciate how the apostolic Church read and prayed the Psalms we need go no further than the fourth chapter of the Acts of the Apostles. Here we learn that Peter and John, who had been boldly preaching in Jerusalem the Gospel of the resurrected Messiah, the Lord Jesus, had been brought before the supreme law court of the Jews, the Sanhedrin, and told to stop preaching. On their release Peter and John returned to the fellowship of believers who began to praise the Lord in prayer.

They lifted up their voice to God with one accord and said, "Lord, thou art God, which hast made heaven and earth, and the sea, and all that in them is. Who by the mouth of thy servant David has said, 'Why did the heathen rage and the people imagine vain things? The kings of the earth stood up, and the rulers were gathered together against the Lord and against his Christ.' [Ps.2:1-2] For of a truth against thy holy child, Jesus, whom thou hast anointed, both Herod, and Pontius Pilate, with the Gentiles, and the people of Israel, were gathered together..."

We notice that the early Christian fellowship, gathered in prayer, interprets the hostile kings and rulers of Psalm 2 in terms of Herod and Pontius Pilate, and the opposing "heathen" and "people" as the Gentiles (represented by the Roman empire), and the Jews. The "his Christ" or "his Anointed One" is understood as referring to Jesus himself (v.27). The primitive, apostolic Church interpreted Psalm 2 not only as a prophecy concerning Jesus as the Messiah but also concerning the suffering of His ambassadors (Church) in the world as they proclaim His Gospel.

So it was that the Church came, by the example of Christ and through the illumination of His Spirit, to see in the Psalms both the vocation and experience of Christ and the vocation and experience of His Church. These are the two sides of the one divine coin and the two parts of one, whole approach. The Psalter as a whole is the prayer of the Church as the Body of Christ and further, it is the prayer of both Head and Body (with all its members), that is of Christ and His brethren. The Epistle to the Hebrews teaches us to think of Christ as our exalted High Priest who as our Mediator in the presence of God is also our Intercessor there. When we pray in His name we are joined in the Spirit with His prayer which He continually offers to the praise of God and for the good of His people. Thus to pray the Psalter in and with Him as His Body is to be joined to Him in His priestly, heavenly prayer.

Perhaps no-one has expressed all this spiritual truth and insight more delightfully and accurately than St Augustine of Hippo in his opening comments on Psalm 86 in his famous *Commentary* or *Ennarations* on the Psalms. His train of thought is compact and thus needs to be read slowly and carefully, for it has refrence not only to praying the Psalter but also the whole Divine Office:

No greater gift could God have given to men than in making His Word, by which He created all things, their Head, and joining them to Him as His members: that the Son of God might become also the Son of man, one God with the Father, one Man with men; so that when we speak to God [the Father] in prayer for mercy, we do not separate the Son from Him; and when the Body of the Son prays, it separates not its Head from itself: and it is the one Saviour of His Body, our Lord Jesus Christ, the Son of God, who both prays for us, and prays in us, and is prayed to by us. He prays for us, as our Priest: He prays in us, as our Head; He is prayed to by us, as our God. Let us therefore recognize in Him our words and His words in us.

And a little later he said:

Therefore we pray to Him, through Him, in Him; and we speak with Him, and He speaks with us; we speak in Him, He speaks in us the prayer of this psalm, which is entitled "A Prayer of David."

So via the Psalter and in its inspired words we pray to the Father through the Son and the Son prays in us to the Father.

In the rest of this chapter we shall note first of all how the Psalms in Christian use become that prayer which rises from His Body (and each and every member) in and through Christ, our Head, to the Father; and then, secondly, we shall see how they are also the prayer of Christ, our heavenly Priest, both in us and for us.

Perhaps I need to make clear (as I did in a chapter on the Psalms in my *Meditating as a Christian*) that it is wise for us today to build the spiritual, Christocentric reading of the Psalms on what is called the historical-grammatical study of them. Not all the Fathers felt this need but we, living in a different world where the study of history is part of our cultural heritage and mindset, need to pay attention to the historical situation in Israel before we move on to the spiritual situation of the new Israel. Again it is a matter of the informative reading preceding and proceeding to the formative. To achieve this purpose I commend Tremper Longmann III, *How to read the Psalms*, 1988, along with Donald Kidner, *The Psalms*, 1975.

In and through Him

Jesus was a Jewish male and thus in and through Him, as members of His Body, we are united with His people, the Jews or Israelites. Israel's history and experience under the old covenant becomes through Jesus the history and experience of the Church under the new covenant. So it is foolish, to say the least, to omit the names Israel or Zion from the Psalter - as some modern church psalters do, for political reasons. Our God is the God of Noah, Abraham, Moses, David and Elijah! And we read the record of God's dealings with the Israelites from the perspective of the fulfillment of the Old Testament by Jesus Christ, who came not to destroy the law of Moses and the contents of the prophecies of the Prophets but to bring them to fulfillment. We assume that the New is in the Old concealed and the Old is by the New revealed and Jesus Christ is the key to both Testaments.

The apostle Paul states this with his usual clarity when he calls the people of the new covenant by the term, "the Israel of God" (Gal.6:17) and claims that this people has inherited the wonderful promises made to the old Israel (see Gal. 3:6ff. & 4:21ff.). However, he makes it clear in Romans

..1 that the Church is not the replacement of Israel but the embodiment of Israel until "the times of the Gentiles be fulfilled." The old Israel is the olive tree, many of whose branches have been cut off through unbelief, and the Church composed of the Gentile peoples is a wild olive grafted into the old olive tree, whose roots go down into Abraham. Being in the olive tree all the branches, both Jew and non-Jew (Gentile), are fed from the same trunk—thus their history is one, that of the Israel of God recorded in the Old Testament. So the Old Testament is the first part of the Christian Bible, and it is precisely this, the Christian Bible. Its only meaning for Christianity as a living religion in terms of the logic of faith is that meaning which Jesus, the Christ, gives it.

In practice, this means that in reading and praying the Psalms each day Christian believers interpret them through Christ, that is in the light of the life, death, and resurrection of Jesus Christ and the teaching from the Holy Spirit of His apostles. So, for example, there are not a few Psalms and parts of Psalms which praise God the Creator and Sustainer of the universe. By His almighty word each and every part of the cosmos is kept in being and motion (see e.g. Psalms 8, 19, 95, & 104) and everything He has made praises Him. In the New Testament we learn that God the Father created and sustains the universe by the eternal Son (the eternal Word) and through the Holy Spirit (see John 1:3 & Col.1:16). The Word which God utters and which both brings everything into being and keeps everything in being is the Son himself. So Christians allow this doctrinal teaching to enter their praying of the Psalms and thus their use of them is in and through Christ. The created order reveals the glory of the Father, the Son and the Holy Spirit.

There is much in the Psalms about the history of the people and tribes of Israel. In particular there is emphasis upon the Exodus from Egypt and in a lesser manner upon the Exile of the tribes in Babylon (see Psalms 95, 106, & 136). Included in the Exodus is the deliverance from bondage, the receiving of the Law at Sinai, the wilderness wanderings and the final entry into Canaan, the land of promise and the land of milk and honey. Prayed in and with Christ the Exodus points to the mighty act of God in the deliverance of his people through the Cross and Resurrection of Jesus: as the old covenant was brought into being by the Exodus so the new is created by the new Exodus of Calvary. The giving of the Law as the expression of the covenant relationship at Sinai points to the giving of the new Law by Jesus on the hill in Palestine where he delivered the Sermon on the Mount (Matt. 5-7). Jesus is the new and greater Moses! The wanderings in the wilderness are the symbol of the journey both of the Church as the community in covenant with God and the Christian soul in a personal relation with God on the way to the kingdom of God in the age to come. And, finally, the promised land of milk and honey points to the goal of the earthly journey, the fullness of everlasting life in the beatific vision of God through Jesus Christ in heaven itself.

The Exile of the sixth century B.C. was an extremely painful experience for the tribes of Israel for it led to the virtual loss of ten of them and the chastisement by God of the two which remained. The story is told in the last part of 2 Kings and the pain is expressed in parts of the writings of the Prophets (e.g. in Jeremiah and Ezekiel). Psalms 79 captures this experience of horror and pain, "O God the heathen are come into thine inheritance; thy holy temple have they defiled." Praying such Psalms in Christ the Church intercedes for those of its members who suffer for the cause of Christ and are persecuted for His name. It also enters into the pain resulting from chastisement when God chooses to purify His new covenant people through suffering on the way of sanctification. Thus in praying these Psalms one part of the Church of God identifies with and empathizes with another part and in so doing enters into the union of Christ with His suffering disciples.

It is not surprising that the Psalms have much to say about the glorious Temple, built by Solomon, as the House of God and the city of Jerusalem, captured by his father,

David, and made the "City of God." Psalms 24, 47 and 48 refer to the Temple on Mount Zion. Prayed through Christ the Temple becomes the very Body of Jesus himself. (See John 2:21 where John tells us that Jesus spoke of His own Body as the new Temple of God and see also 1 Corinthians 3:16-17 and 6:19 where Paul declares that the Church of the new covenant is the new Temple of the Holy Spirit.) God is present with and unto His new covenant people by His indwelling of them and thus where they are gathered in the name of the Lord Jesus there is God's own Temple. Further, the old city of Jerusalem on Mount Zion to which Psalms 48 and 102 refer points in Christ to the new Jerusalem which is the mother of the faithful (so Paul in Gal. 4:26) and which, according to the glorious vision of John in Revelation 21-22, is the community of heaven itself with Christ as its very center (see also Heb. 12:22). Thus, prayed in Christ, Jerusalem is the Church of God, triumphant and perfected in Christ in heaven; it is also the very Church which is still militant with Christ again sin and death on earth. And within this context of understanding those Psalms (e.g 113 to 118) which speak of the festivals and pilgrimages of Israel are used with reference to the great festivals of the Church - Easter and Pentecost.

The Psalms which the devout have always found difficult to fit into this Christian use are the few which are often called the imprecatory Psalms (see 94 & 109), which call upon God to execute His vengeance upon the wicked and the enemies of Israel. Thus in some modern editions of the Psalter such Psalms are sometimes omitted or the parts of Psalms which are judged to breathe this vengeance are bracketed so that they can be omitted. However, if the Church is praying these Psalms in and through Christ she is praying them through the One whose sacrificial self-offering and Atonement absorbed the wrath of God against wickedness - in fact absorbed God's wrath against all sin. By Christ we are saved from the wrath of God (Rom.5:9). Therefore, while God must by His very holy nature be opposed to and punish all wickedness and evil, He has made it possible for sinners of all kinds to be saved from His wrath since He has provided the means in the sacrificial death of Jesus for His wrath to be turned into mercy towards repentant sinners. To pray these Psalms in Christ is to pray them through the very One whom God the Father "set forth to be a propitiation through faith in his blood" (Rom.3:25).

Of course many of the Psalms easily become Christian prayers without too much meditative effort by those who use them (e.g. Psalms 27 & 28) for the LORD who is there named is known to Christians either as the Lord Jesus Christ or the One God, who is the Father, the Son and the Holy Spirit. Then their accurate statement of the human condition and their cries to God for help and mercy convert quickly into the prayers of those believers who find themselves sorely tried and tempted in this world and are seeking God's help and guidance (e.g. Psalms 42 and 51) to live the Christian life. Further, the hymns of praise immediately become Christian hymns of praise (e.g. Psalms 33 and 111-113) as God is again understood as the One who is revealed and has acted in Jesus Christ, the Lord. And the Psalms (especially 119) which thank God for His Law and Word become testimonies and prayers to Jesus Christ, the Word made flesh and the giver of the new Law.

The experience of the centuries is that practice makes perfect! This approach to the Psalter takes time to develop and is a process of prayer which is never exhausted or completed in this life. The Lord is forever surprising His covenant children who pray to Him as the Body of Christ in the prayers of the Psalter.

From the Son to the Father

In the Psalter there is a set of Psalms which have been called the Royal Psalms (see e.g. Psalms 2, 18, 20, 21 & 45). They are addressed to the king as petitionary prayers or thanksgivings; sometimes they express his prayer, or present a royal processional song or a bridal ode for his marriage.

Within these Psalms the king is the "son of God" and seemingly excessive claims are made for his reign and his kingdom. He is the "anointed one of the LORD" who will bring peace and justice to the world and save his own people. Developing from the use Jesus himself and his apostles made of Psalm 110, which is the most quoted psalm in the New Testament (see its use in Matthew 22:41ff.), the early Church came to view this and the other messianic Psalms in terms of Christ calling out to the Father and/or the Father speaking to the Son. Psalm 110 has only seven verses but it is pregnant with meaning and begins with the LORD God telling the Messiah-king to sit at His right hand, the highest place of honor and majesty. The king is then promised by God that his enemies will become his footstool and that he will rule over a willing, obedient people. Further, he will not only continue as king but as priest, a unique priesthood that of Melchizedek (for whom see Gen.14:8 & Heb.5:6ff; 7:1ff). Thus to read and pray these royal Psalms as prophecies of Christ in his relationship to the Father is to enter by faith into the relationship of the Son to the Father. It is to come to the Father in and through Jesus Christ and participate both in His kingdom of grace and His communion with the Father.

To take a few examples from the royal Psalms. Originally Psalm 72 probably referred to Solomon as "the king's son"—David's son. In Christian use it became a prayer that the kingdom of the Son of God would extend over the whole earth—"yea, all kings shall fall down before Him; all nations shall serve Him." In contrast, Psalm 144 is a prayer of an Israelite king who gives thanks to God for victory in battle and then asks for blessings upon his people. In Christian use it became the prayer of Christ thanking God the Father for His victory over sin, death and hell and asking that His Church and kingdom would prosper.

Psalm 45 addresses the king, the Lord God and then the new queen, in celebration of the marriage of the king to the queen. In Christian use it was seen as portraying the mystical marriage between Christ, the Bridegroom, and the Church, the Bride (see Eph. 5:32).

Much more could be said about the Psalter. I close this section with a Latin expression which captures the traditional Christian use of the Psalms: *semper in ore psalmus, semper in corde Christus* (always a psalm on the lips, always Christ in the heart).

Wisdom from Bishop George Horne

[Below are three quotations from the Preface to his *Commentary;* the first is from page i, the second from page vi and the third from page xvii of the 1836 edition.]

1. [On the greatness of the Psalter] The Psalms are an epitome of the Bible, adapted to the purposes of devotion. They treat occasionally of the creation and formation of the world; the dispensations of providence and the economy of grace; the transaction of the patriarchs; the exodus of the children of Israel; their journey through the wilderness and settlement in Canaan; their law, priesthood and ritual; the exploits of their great men, wrought through faith; their sins and captivities; their repentances and restorations; the sufferings and victories of David; the peaceful and happy reign of Solomon; the advent of the Messiah with its effects and consequences; His incarnation, birth, life, passion, death, resurrection, ascension, kingdom, and priesthood; the effusion of the Spirit; the conversion of the nations; the rejection of the Jews; the establishment, increase and perpetuity of the Christian Church; the end of the world; the general judgment; the condemnation of the wicked, and the final triumph of the righteous with their Lord and King. These are the subjects here presented to our meditations.

We are instructed how to conceive of them aright, and to express the different affections, which, when so conceived of, they must excite in our minds. They are, for this purpose, adorned with the figures, and set off with all the graces of poetry; and poetry itself is designed yet farther to be recommended by the charms of music, thus consecrated to the service of God; that so delight may prepare the way for improvement, and pleasure become the handmaid of wisdom, while every turbulent passion is calmed by sacred melody, and the evil spirit is still dispossessed by the harp of the son of Jesse. This little volume, like the paradise of Eden, affords us in perfection, though in a miniature, everything that groweth elsewhere, "every tree that is pleasant to the sight and good for food:" and, above all, what was there lost, but is here restored, the *tree of life in the midst of the garden.* That which we read, as a matter of speculation, in other Scriptures, is reduced to practice, when we recite it in the Psalms; in those, repentance and faith are described, but in these, they are acted; by a perusal of the former, we learn how others served God, but, by using the latter, we serve him ourselves.

2. [Spiritual interpretation is open to over development and thus to be abused.] That the spiritual interpretation of the Scripture, like all other good things, is liable to abuse, and that it hath been actually abused, both in ancient and modern days, cannot be denied. He who shall go about to apply, in this way, any passage, before he hath attained its literal meaning, may say what in itself is pious and true; but foreign to the text from which he endeavoureth to introduce it. St Jerome, it is well known, when grown older and wiser, lamented that, in the fervours of a youthful fancy, he had spiritualized the prophecy of Obadiah, before he understood (its historical, literal meaning). And it must be allowed, that a due attention to the occasion and scope of the Psalms would have pared off many unseemly excrescences, which now deform the commentaries of St Augustine and other Fathers, upon them. But these and other concessions of the same kind being made, as they are made very freely, men of sense will consider, that a principle is not therefore to be rejected, because it has been abused, since human errors can never invalidate the truths of God.

3. [On the Christian interpretation of the Psalms.] As God is ever the same, and his doings uniform, his conduct towards mankind must exactly be proportioned to his conduct towards the Jewish nation. Let us therefore place God in common over them both; and there will be on the one side, the Jewish nation; and on the other, mankind: on the one side, Canaan, and a national prosperity; on the other heaven and human happiness: on one side, a redemption from Egyptian servitude and national evils; on the other, a redemption of the whole human race from absolute evil: on the one side, national crimes atoned by national ceremonies, sacrifices, priests; on the other, sins expiated by the one universal sacrifice of Jesus Christ: on one side, national and temporary saviours, kings, prophets and judges; on the other, all this universal and eternal: on one side, the law, and every branch of it, adapted to a favourite nation; on the other, the everlasting gospel suited to all mankind.

It is impossible, therefore, that God can say anything to David, under the quality of king of this chosen nation, which he does not speak, at the same time, to Jesus Christ, as King of all the elect; and that in a truer and nobler sense. To each of them he speaks in a sense adapted to the nature of their respective kingdoms. Nor is this latter a bare accommodation of words, but the first and highest meaning of them, and which only, absolutely speaking, can be the true sense of God; the other being this sense, confined to a particular circumstance; in other words, an absolute truth, made history, and matter of fact. This is a principle, which shows, that far from denying the Christian application, I consider the literal and historical sense only as a kind of vehicle for it.

8

HOLY COMMUNION

We have seen that through His Gospel, God calls us into a relationship with Himself as the Triune Lord in which He is the bountiful giver of all that is good for us for time and eternity. In Baptism we enter this covenant of grace; in Confirmation we are strengthened and promise to be faithful as members of the Church of God and as the covenant partners of the LORD; and in the Daily Offices we recognize what this membership and partnership means through confessing our sins, praising the Lord our God, hearing His Word and offering our petitions and intercessions to Him.

Through hearing and meditating upon His Word and in the dynamic encounter with God which the Daily Office allows, believers enjoy communion with God through Jesus Christ, their Lord. This daily and continuing encounter is intended by the Common Prayer Tradition to be intimately related to the unique encounter with God which He provides in "The Order for the Administration of the Lord's Supper." Holy Communion is the weekly, supernatural meal of the new covenant; it is the unique, spiritual food provided from heaven by the Lord our God for His covenant people on each Lord's Day as well as on special holy days (and indeed whenever they gather in His name and for His glory to celebrate the Lord's Supper). Yet it is a feast for which the covenant people of God must prepare so that they are truly ready to receive such supernatural and heavenly food.

The Communion is with the Triune Lord through the incarnate Son, Jesus Christ, who is the only Mediator between God and mankind. Only because the Son as true God took to Himself from the Virgin Mary our human nature and flesh and satisfied the demands of the law of God in our place, even to the extent of offering Himself as the sacrifice for our sins, have we, as sinners, any right to come to God at all. In Holy Communion as believing sinners we are so marvelously united by the Holy Spirit with the exalted Lord Jesus, who died for us, that we are enabled to participate in and truly benefit from His full redemption of our bodies and souls.

Thus in the Catechism we are taught that in this Sacrament "the inward part, or thing signified, is the Body and Blood of Christ, which are spiritually taken and received by the faithful." Further we learn that "the benefits whereof we are partakers in the Lord's Supper are the strengthening and refreshing of our souls by the Body and Blood of Christ as our bodies are strengthened and refreshed by the Bread and Wine."

The logic of faith

As put together by Archbishop Cranmer in 1549/52 the Lord's Supper has the same basic structure - the logic of faith —as the Daily Office. In the first part, called the Ante-Communion (based on the "Liturgy of the Catechumens" in the early Church), there is an introductory sequence of this logic of faith. The worshippers move from the recognition before God of their sinfulness by hearing God's holy law, first to the hearing of the mercy and grace of God in the two readings (Epistle and Gospel) from the New Testament and the proclamation of good news in the sermon, and then, secondly, to the expression and responsiveness of faith in the Creed and Prayer for the "whole state of Christ's Church."

In the second part, once called the "Liturgy of the Faithful," there is the same sequence but in a different and deeper way. "All that do truly and earnestly repent you of your sins..." are invited to draw near with faith, confess their sins to God and take the holy Sacrament so as to receive divine comfort and spiritual sustenance. Then follows the Absolution and the hearing of the comforting (comfortable) promises and assurances of God's grace to penitent sinners. Step three is thanksgiving for salvation, faith responding to divine grace and celebrating that heavenly mercy. In the *Sursum Corda*, therefore, the forgiven, praising, covenant people of God lift up their hearts and give thanks as they are joined in the Holy Spirit to the heavenly choir who magnify and glorify the Name of the Lord our God.

Faith is now expectant and the souls are ready to be fed by heavenly manna from the Table of the Lord. In the consecrated bread and wine, which is the sacramental body and blood of the Lord Jesus who died but is alive for evermore, God ministers to His covenant people by spiritually feeding them as they are in union with Himself in the Body of Christ with the gracious salvation which He has already proclaimed to them in the gospel words of assurance and mercy. Receiving the sacramental body and blood of Christ is thus the summit of responsive faith. It is being united with the Lord of glory, who once died on Calvary to make Atonement for sin, so that what He is and possesses now in heaven is shared with His people. Having been nourished and having been allowed to enter into intimate knowing/communion with their Lord at His heavenly table, the covenant people of God then go forth into daily life to "continue in that holy fellowship and do all such good works as God has prepared for them to walk in." Thus Liturgy is for life: knowing God is to be the basis of the daily vocation.

Over the centuries the Cranmerian basic structure of the double and deepening logic of faith of this Service has been modified (some would say enriched) in the revisions of the Common Prayer Tradition. However, the basic biblical logic of personal confession of sin, the announcement to penitents of forgiveness and grace, and the response of faith to what God graciously offers in Jesus Christ by the Holy Spirit is still much in evidence in all Books of Common Prayer up to the Canadian Book of 1962. Since then there has been a constant chorus of criticism of the Common Prayer Tradition accusing it of majoring too much on sin, guilt and justification by grace. This chorus is informed less by new Bible study and more by contemporary secular studies, which have little or no place for the view of sin and a holy God presented by our Lord and His apostles and believed in the Church over many centuries. We need always to remember that human beings are not merely rebels against God who need to stop their rebellion and be forgiven, they are also diseased sinners who need an internal cure from the heavenly Physician and Saviour! They need to be lifted out of the power of the old epoch/age which is dominated by sin and death and placed into the new epoch/age in Christ wherein is everything that God has planned for them. Thus it is the new creation not the old creation which lies at the heart of this Service. It is the celebration of the new creation in, with and by Christ in the power of the Holy Spirit in the presence of God the Father.

Sacrament of the New Covenant

There are accounts of the institution of the Lord's Supper in three Gospels (Matt.26:26ff; Mark 14:22ff; Luke 22:14ff) as well as by Paul (1 Cor. 11:23ff). We learn from them that the new covenant, that is the new, everlasting relationship of fellowship and communion between God and man in Christ Jesus, was inaugurated by the bloody sacrifice of atonement which Jesus offered in His death upon the Cross of Calvary. Thus at the Last Supper He referred to the cup of wine as "my blood of the new testament [covenant] shed for the remission of sins" and to the bread which He broke as "my body broken for you."

This means that the primary reference of the Liturgy of the Lord's Supper can only be the sacrificial, atoning death of Christ Jesus at Calvary, and what this Atonement achieved for God's creatures, who stand in need of being reconciled to Him and redeemed by Him. Certainly Jesus took the fruit of the old creation, the wheatbread and the wine, and used them as the effectual signs and symbols of the new creation; but, the emphasis is not upon the old creation as such but upon the new—the kingdom of God of the new epoch or age. Of this glorious future kingdom, to be known in full after the Second Coming of Jesus Christ in glory, we experience only the firstfruits now in anticipation of the total and never-ending fruit in the fullness of the life of the kingdom to come.

Thus being invited to the Lord's Supper and eating at His table is to receive a taste of the food of the kingdom of God to come. It is to be given a preliminary place at the heavenly Messianic banquet. It is to be fed now with that spiritual and heavenly manna which will sustain the life of the redeemed, new creation in heaven for all eternity. The body and blood of Jesus, the heavenly Lord who died for our sins and rose for our justification, are truly heavenly, nourishing food to our souls and bodies for by them we are incorporated more fully and intimately into His mystical Body. We are jointed to Him as our Lord and Mediator, King and Physician, Master and Saviour. And in, through and by Him we come to the Father. Yet this spiritual and heavenly banquet is only open to repentant, believing souls. There are dire warnings both given by Paul (1 Cor.11:27ff.) and written into the three Exhortations provided for use in *BCP* (1928) concerning coming to the Table of the Lord without having first made suitable, spiritual and moral preparation.

Happily the Common Prayer Tradition does not fix one particular way of explaining how the risen and exalted Lord Jesus Christ, who once died for us, is actually present in the celebration of the Lord's Supper. Of course He has promised always to be with His people —"Lo I am with you alway, even unto the end of the world"—and so he is present through the Holy Spirit, His Paraclete or Comforter (John 14-16), at all church services. Nevertheless, there is a special, covenanted presence promised to the believing people of the new covenant when they meet at His holy Table to eat His body and drink His blood. In a manner which defies final description He is specifically present in the breaking and eating of bread and the pouring and drinking of wine for He makes them His own body and blood unto those who are united to Him in faith and love. Those who come with penitent and believing hearts to his Table do not need to offer Him an explanation of how the Sacrament works; it works for their salvation and they increase in the knowing of their Lord not by the exercise of their understanding or ingenuity but by His supernatural grace.

Perhaps Queen Elizabeth I was not far wrong in her theology in the following quatrain that she is reputed to have composed:

He was the Word that spake it,

He took the bread and brake it;

And what that Word did make it,

I do believe and take it.

Faithful reception at this Sacrament and means of grace includes a basic, simple faith as is expressed here by the Queen.

Bearing this in mind, those who are walking with God and confessing Jesus as Lord in their daily lives ought to approach the Table of the Lord each Lord's Day. It is entirely appropriate that the Lord's people be at the Lord's Table on the Lord's Day, the day of resurrection and of the future kingdom of God. They should rejoice to be invited to attend His Messianic Feast on each anniversary of his Resurrection in order to know that their sins are forgiven, that they are reconciled to God in Christ, that unto them is given the taste and the promise of everlasting life, and that they have a vocation from God on this earth now in this sinful epoch. Thereby the Liturgy is truly liturgy for life for they are sent forth from the Banquet to serve God in His world. Likewise, whenever possible the people of the new covenant should be present at his Table on the major feast days (for which see chapter nine below).

A Comparison

Though the *BCP* (1928) and *BCP* (1962) belong to the same Common Prayer Tradition, they present in their Services for Holy Communion two differing forms. The Canadian Book may be traced back to the English *BCP* (1662) in a straight line; in contrast, the American Book can only be traced back to the English *BCP* (1662) via the input of the English Non-Jurors of the late seventeenth century and of the Scottish Episcopal Church of the eighteenth century. The major difference between the two is in the Prayer of Consecration.

The American Prayer addresses the Father in "the Oblation" in these words: " we do celebrate and make before thy Divine Majesty, with these thy holy gifts, which we now offer unto thee, the memorial thy Son hath commanded us to make." The key words are "which we now offer unto thee," which are not in the *BCP* (1662) or its successors. This clause comes from the Scottish Service of 1764. The thinking behind its inclusion is that there must be oblation in connection with remembrance. Cranmer had removed the oblation because of its association in the late medieval period with the idea of the Mass as a propitiatory sacrifice, offered to God for the removal of sin. The replacement of the act of oblation was intended to recover what was done in the early Church when the offering of the holy gifts to God was seen not as a propitiatory sacrifice but as the offering of prayer, praises and the "holy gifts" of bread and wine.

Following the Oblation the American Prayer has "the Invocation" wherein the merciful Father is asked "to bless and sanctify, with thy Word and Holy Spirit these thy gifts and creatures of bread and wine." Here the Second and Third Persons of the One Godhead are understood to effect that gracious work whereby those who receive the consecrated bread and wine receive the Body and Blood of Christ. This invocation is not in the *BCP* (1662) and its successors.

There is one further difference to note. The Lord's Prayer is presented in *BCP* (1928) as the climax of the Prayer of Consecration and thus comes before the Prayer of Humble Access ("We do not presume..."). In contrast the Lord's Prayer is said immediately after the Communion in the *BCP* (1662 & 1962).

Some would argue that the additions to the Common Prayer Tradition in the Scottish and American Books bring the Prayer of Consecration more into line with the earlier Liturgy of the Church before the medieval period and thereby make it a more satisfactory Prayer.

Reflections

(i)The logic of faith of the Order for the "Administration of the Lord's Supper" requires for its full expression and development biblical preaching. This is the divinely-appointed means of grace whereby God's Word addresses those who have gathered and brings them deeper in understanding and feeling to their Lord. So the sermon is hardly the place for a discussion of the latest politics or social problems: these can be considered at other times and in other places. Though there are many different ways of preaching, for God's Word comes through a human personality, yet there is only one basic content in preaching—a message from God and of God to God's people. It is a message from heaven addressed to earth; it is glad tidings of the kingdom of God addressed to the kingdoms of this world; it is the gospel of salvation addressed to needy sinners.

(ii)The Canadian Book (1962), unlike the *BCP* (1662), includes between the Prayer of Consecration and the Prayer of Humble Access what has come to be called "the Peace". However, it is said in the context of the whole congregation kneeling and thus there is no possibility of people moving around to greet or hug friends. This stands in contrast to the way "the Peace" has come to be understood and practised since the appearance of the new Books.

In the new Books "the Peace" is placed between the Ministry of the Word and the Celebration of the Sacrament and it is intended to be an important part of the Service. Normally people are encouraged to move about and greet one another in ways they deem appropriate. This is done in order, it is stated, to accord with ancient practice, as far as this is known. The Canadian *BAS* (1985) offers an explanatory note on what is "the Peace." It is "an encounter, a reconciliation, and an anticipation." As an encounter it allows the worshippers "to meet Christ in others"; as a reconciliation it dramatizes the injunction of Matthew 5:23-24" (to be reconciled to your brother before bringing your gift to the altar); and as an anticipation "it dramatizes the eucharist as a foretaste of the banquet of the kingdom" through the experience of peace and unity.

These are noble thoughts but for their realization modern Eucharistic assemblies must compare favorably with those of the Early Church, whose practice of sharing "the kiss of peace" (Rom.16:16; 1 Cor. 16:20; 2 Cor. 13:12; 1 Thess. 5:26 & 1 Pet.:14) was much more than an "hello" or "how are you?" Too often today "the Peace" becomes the focal point of the Service and is the place where people (out of the individualistic ethos of modern life) affirm one another without reference to the ethos and teaching and demands of the Gospel of Christ. I have sometimes said that it easily becomes the sacrament of pantheism or panentheism—affirming God's presence in and through each other and thus affirming each other. Many people obviously seem to enjoy the experience of greeting each other; however. whether it is appropriate or true to the Gospel as currently practised is another matter. It surely ought only to be done if and only if it truly makes a contribution to the purpose of the assembling together—to meet the Lord Jesus, to hear His Word and to be fed at His Table with His Body and Blood.

Regrettably, in the *BCP* (1979) the Rite 1 Holy Communion which is in traditional language and which is intended to reflect the *BCP* (1928) tradition places "the exchange of the Peace" between the Ministry of the Word and the Ministry of the Sacrament, thereby making Rite 1 conform to the structure of Rite II, the modern version. However, there is a note in the "Additional Directions" which states that "if preferred the exchange of the Peace may take place at the time of the administration of the Sacrament (before or after the sentence of Invitation)." Yet the way in which the Service is printed makes this possibility into an improbability!

(iii)It seems to me that there is a great need in the parishes to recover a spirit of awe and reverence at and in this holy service. A celebration before God and with the Lord Jesus is not a secular event but is the holy Lord calling His covenant people before Him to share in His holy love. Certainly there is joy, abundant joy, at the Messianic Feast but it is holy joy. Perhaps modern Anglicans should have fewer Holy Communions in order to give themselves opportunity to revive the classic tradition of being able rightly to prepare for attendance at them.

In particular, to think that each time Episcopalians meet they ought to have a Eucharist (which seems to be the modern wisdom in the ECUSA) is to have reduced this holy encounter with the Risen Lord to that of a kind of fast-food or microwave religion. What is wrong with saying the morning or evening office at such gatherings? It is regrettable that the *BCP* (1979) does not have the Exhortations of the *BCP* (1928) and other Books of the Common Prayer Tradition. To all those who wish to attend Holy Communion in order to know their Lord experientially as they feed on His Body and Blood I strongly recommend the regular reading of one or more of these Exhortations as part of the preparation for attendance. They may be old-fashioned but they address the soul!

Wisdom from Christopher Sutton

[In reading Anglican writers over the years I have noticed the great respect many had for the writings of Christopher Sutton, a canon of Winchester Cathedral. Here is an excerpt from his much read book, *Godly Meditations upon the Most Holy Sacrament of the Lord's Supper,* 1613.]

This is the marriage feast of the King of heaven: the Banquet is spiritual, whose bread doth strengthen man's heart and whose wine doth inflame the soul with heavenly joy; and the meat thereof is the flesh of Christ, who says. "My flesh is meat indeed." This is that healthful food of angels sent down from heaven, having in it all delight and savoury sweetness. This is that fat bread which giveth pleasures for a king. This is the most plentiful bread of good nourishment above all that earth yieldeth. This is the bread of the offering of the first fruits. This is the bread signified as well in the cakes, which Abraham did set before the angels, as also in the shewbread; and this was likewise revealed in the bread and wine which Melchizedek brought forth. Lastly, this is the bread baked upon the coals in the strength whereof Elisha did walk forty days and forty nights unto Horeb, the mount of God. This is that tree of life, planted by the Almighty God in the midst of the earthly paradise. whose fruit being eaten would preserve bodily life. This is that Paschal Lamb without spot, by whose blood dabbed upon the two posts and the lintel of the door, the children of Israel were in times past delivered from the hand of the angel that smote the Egyptians. This is that kid which Manoah offered unto the Lord upon the stone. This is also that honeycomb which Jonathan, dipping the tip of his rod therein, did put to his mouth and his eyes were enlightened. This is also that large flowing stream of water which suddenly issued out of the rock after Moses had stricken it with his rod.

Come freely therefore to this most sweet Banquet of Christ Jesus wherein is promised unto thee most assured life and salvation... Oh therefore, faithful soul, if thou be unclean, come to the foutain of purity; if thou be hungry, come and feed of the bread of life which fadeth not and filleth the hungry soul with goodness. Art thou sick? This will be a most sovereign medicine for thine infirmity... Art thou sorrowful and in perplexity? This wine doth make joyful the inward man. Do many things trouble thee? Cleave fast to Him who calmed the waves of the sea when they were troubled. Goest thou astray from the Lord and Master? Yet mayest thou walk in the strength of this meat, even to the Mount of God...

Theology from Samuel Seabury

[Bishop Seabury has left us a well argued theology of the Holy Eucharist in his Discourse VI in *Discourse on Several Subjects* (vol.1. 1815). In this extract he explains the logic of the Prayer of Consecration of *BCP* (1928).]

At the time of the celebration, the officiating bishop or priest, first gives thanks to God for all his mercies, especially for those of creation and redemption. Then, to show the authority by which he acts, and his obedience to the command of Christ, he recites the institution of the holy sacrament which he is celebrating, as the holy evangelists have recorded it. In doing this, he takes the bread into his hands and breaks it, to represent the dead body of Christ, torn and pierced on the cross; the cup also, of wine and water mixed, representing the blood and water which flowed from the dead body of Christ, when wounded by the soldier's spear. Over the bread and the cup he repeats Christ's powerful words, THIS IS MY BODY, THIS IS MY BLOOD.

The elements being thus made authoritative representations, or symbols of Christ's crucified body and blood, are in a proper capacity to be offered to God as the great and acceptable sacrifice of the Christian Church. Accordingly, the oblation, which is the highest, most solemn, and proper act of Christian worship, is then immediately made. Continuing his prayer, the priest intercedes with the Almighty

Father to send upon them (the bread and wine) the Holy Spirit, to sanctify and bless them and make the *bread* the *body* and the *cup* the *blood* of Christ—his spiritual life-giving body and blood in power and virtue; that, to all the faithful, they may be effectual to all spiritual purposes. Nor does he cease his prayer and oblation, till he has interceded for the whole catholic church, and all the members of it; concluding all in the name and through the merit of Jesus Christ, the Saviour.

The Eucharist being, as its name imparts, a sacrifice of thanksgiving, the bread and wine, after they have been offered or given to God, and blessed and sanctified by his Holy Spirit, are returned to the hand of his minister to be eaten by the faithful, as a *feast upon the sacrifice*—the priest first partaking of them himself, and then distributing them to the communicants; to denote their being at peace and favour with God, being thus fed at his table, and eating of his food; and also to convey to the worthy receivers all the benefits and blessings of Christ's natural body and blood, which were offered and slain for their redemption.

For this reason the Eucharist is also called the communion of the body and blood of Christ; not only because, by communing together, we declare our mutual good will and our unity in the church and faith of Christ; but also, because, in that holy ordinance we communicate with God through Christ the Mediator, by first offering, or giving to him the sacred symbols of the body and blood of his dear Son, and then receiving them again, blessed and sanctified by his Holy Spirit, to feast upon at his table, for the refreshment of our souls; for the increase of our faith and hope; for the pardon of our sins; for the renewing of our minds in holiness, by the operation of the Holy Ghost; and for a principle of immortality to our bodies, as well to our souls.

From this consideration, the necessity of frequently communicating in the Holy Eucharist evidently appears. It is the highest act of Christian worship; a direct acknowledgment of God's sovereignty and dominion over us and over all his creatures. It is the memorial of the passion and death of our dear Redeemer, made before the Almighty Father, to render him propitious to us, by pleading with him the meritorious sufferings of his beloved Son, when he made his soul an offering for sin. It is a sensible pledge of God's love to us, who, as he hath given his Son to die for us, so hath he given his precious body and blood, in the holy Eucharist, to be our spiritual food and sustenance: and as the bread of this world frequently taken is necessary to keep the body in health and vigour; so is this bread of God, frequently received, necessary to preserve the soul in spiritual health and keep the divine life of faith and holiness from becoming extinct in us.

9

THE CHURCH YEAR

We live in space and time, dependent always upon the Lord our God for life. For us day succeeds day, month succeeds month and year succeeds year. We cannot escape time. In contrast, God, who is the Creator of space and time, is above and beyond space and time. He is eternal and infinite Spirit and upon Him space, time and all creatures are dependent. Not only is our God present unto us through space and time but He has also acted decisively for us by revealing Himself in space and time. The center of this revelation is the Incarnation of the eternal Son of God, who took to Himself our human nature and brought salvation, reconciliation and redemption by what He did for us as Jesus, the crucified Messiah. God acted in the specific space of Palestine and the chronological time when the Herods were kings under the protection of the Roman Empire.

The Church Year, beginning on Advent Sunday, exists to facilitate our knowing God as His covenant partners, in dependence upon the ministry of the Holy Spirit. It does so by bringing us within our space and time into constant contact with different dimensions and aspects of the one Mystery, even our Lord Jesus Christ. *Mystery*, the word for God's saving activity in Jesus, is the word Paul often uses, and to appreciate the Church Year as dependent upon and relating to the *Mystery*, we need to note its rich meaning in the Letters of Paul.

Mystery & Mystical

The Greek word, *mysterion*, occurs twenty-seven times in the New Testament and of these twenty occur in the Letters of Paul. Where *mysterion* occurs we find that it is in association with verbs which point to revelation from God or proclamation of the gospel of God. Thus *mysterion* is God's secret, long kept by Him and disclosed by Him through the Holy Spirit to the apostles; in their proclamation of the Gospel and in their teaching this secret is told to all who believe. Believers learn and receive the *mysterion* in order to know the God of mercy and grace in whom they believe, and in particular, by this *mysterion* they know the Lord Jesus Christ.

Paul's reflections upon the *mysterion* begin as he compares God's wisdom and the wisdom of this world in 1 Corinthians 1-2. It is in the Cross, the saving, atoning, redeeming and reconciling activity of the living God in Christ Jesus, that true wisdom is to be found. While the preaching of the Cross appears as foolishness to the secular-minded, to those whose eyes God has opened it is the revelation of heavenly wisdom and the power of salvation. Thus Paul explains: "We speak the wisdom of God in a *mystery*, even the hidden wisdom, which God ordained before the world unto our glory" (2:7).

In the apostolic preaching of the Gospel, the mystery which has been kept a secret by God is proclaimed to the world. Paul makes this clear in the way he ends the Letter to Rome:

Now to him that is of power to stablish you according to my gospel, and the preaching of Jesus Christ, according to the revelation of the mystery which was kept secret since the world began, but now is made manifest, and by the scriptures of the prophets, according to the commandment of the everlasting God, made known to all nations for the obedience of faith: To God only wise, be glory through Jesus Christ for ever. Amen. (16:25-27)

He also asked for prayer that he would preach this *mystery:* "Continue in prayer...that God would open unto us a door of utterance to speak the *mystery* of Christ, for which also I am in bonds" (Col.4:3; see also Eph. 6:19).

By the Gospel God's saving activity in the death of Jesus is revealed: the long-kept secret is manifested. But there is yet more to the *mystery* and Paul gives us the details. He tells the church in Ephesus "how that by revelation God made known unto me the *mystery* ... which in other ages was not made known to the sons of men, as it is now revealed unto his holy apostles and prophets by the Spirit: That the Gentiles should be fellow-heirs, and of the same body, and partakers of the promise in Christ by the gospel: whereof I was made a minister..." (3:4-6). The Gospel of God creates a new humanity in which there will be the reconciliation of Jew and Gentile in one Body, the Body of Christ. This contrasts with the situation under the old covenant when all God's people were of Jewish stock, but it is what God always had in mind. This *mystery* is revealed in the Gospel for by His Cross Christ creates a new people, a new creation, and a new covenant.

There is yet more to the *mysterion*. God's plans call for the internalizing of His grace within the souls of all His new people. Writing to the church in Colossae, Paul speaks of the *mystery* which has been hidden from ages and generations but is now made manifest to his saints and continues: "To whom God would make known what is the riches of the glory of this *mystery* among the Gentiles, which is Christ in you, the hope of glory" (1:27). the indwelling of the Holy Spirit by whom Christ is present in the soul is an aspect of the *mystery* which is first encountered in the Cross of Christ. No wonder Paul can cry out: "I am crucified with Christ, nevertheless I live; yet not I, but Christ liveth in me; and the life I now live in the flesh I live by the faith of the Son of God, who loved me and gave himself for me" (Gal.2:20). It is from this aspect of the *mystery* that we get the true meaning of *mystical*, the experience of God in the soul.

In terms of God's purpose for His creation, there is the cosmic dimension of the *Mysterion*. In the saving deed of Calvary is the power and promise of cosmic regeneration.

To the church in Ephesus, Paul writes: "God hath abounded toward us in all wisdom and prudence, having made known unto us the *mystery* of his will... that in the dispensation of the fullness of times, he might gather together in one all things in Christ, both which are in heaven and which are on earth..." (1:9-11). God's secret, revealed in the Gospel and made possible by Calvary, is to sum up all things in Christ. By Him all things were created and to Him all things will return for their perfection.

Finally, Paul speaks of "the great **mystery**" which is "concerning Christ and the Church" (Eph. 5:32). The intimate union of the people of the new covenant with the Lord Jesus is the great *mysterion*! The Church is the Bride and the Lord Jesus is the Bridegroom and they are bound in *mystical* union.

We may summarize what has been said in one short sentence from Paul: "Great is the *mystery* of godliness" (1 Tim.3:16). It is to this *mystery* or *secret* of God, revealed in the Gospel, that the Church Year points; and in this *mystery* God's covenant people, as the Bride of Christ (who is Lord of the Year) partake during their keeping of the Church Year.

Sunday

In the Ten Commandments God's covenant people were told to "remember the sabbath day, to keep it holy" (Ex.20:8). Since Jesus Christ rose from the dead on the first day of the week, Christians have called this day "the Lord's Day" (Rev. 1:10) and kept it as their day of worship. So instead of the seventh day, Christians meet to hear God's Word and celebrate the Lord's Supper on the first day of the week. They have done this from the very beginning, as the Gospel of John (20:19ff.) and the Acts of the Apostles (20:7ff.) make clear. It is the day when the *mystery* is declared in the Gospel and received in the Sacrament.

In biblical thinking, days, and the week of seven days, belong to the creation of space and time by the Lord God. As Genesis 1 declares, God made the world in six days and rested on the seventh to contemplate what He had made. So the seventh day is the Sabbath and its fulfillment, according to the Letter to the Hebrews, is the sabbath-rest of contemplating God's glory in the kingdom of heaven in the age to come. The fact that Christ rose on the first day and that his Church keeps this day for the worship of Almighty God in His name is a biblical way of proclaiming that by and through the work of Jesus, God has begun a new creation. Further, the first day is also, on a seven day week, the eighth day, and the resurrection of Jesus on this day points to a new start, a new epoch, a new age and a new world centred on the Lord Jesus Christ, the risen and exalted Saviour. You may have noticed that some baptismal fonts have eight sides to declare this truth and to tell the baptized that they enter a new creation by their incorporation into Christ.

Sunday is unique but each day is special for it is a gift from God and an opportunity to meet with God and to serve Him. It is a great comfort to know that the Lord our God does not change and thus His boundless mercy is constant. We can always rely upon Him even if we cannot trust our own feelings and thoughts. In the Daily Office we encounter the *mystery* through the written Word. The Old Testament points forward to Christ crucified for us and for our salvation, and the New Testament proclaims the *mystery* in all its manifold meaning and application to our lives. In meditation we ponder and consider the *mystery* and in contemplation we encounter the *mystery* "Christ in you, the hope of glory." This discipline of prayer is sustained by the monthly cycle of psalms as we pray in and with Christ who is the *Mystery* Himself.

Christmas

There are two major moments in the Christian Year, Easter and Christmas. In connection with each Festival there are special days before and afterwards.

Though there is no certainty that Jesus was born on December 25, the Church has kept this as the date of his birth for a long time. It is the celebration of the Incarnation, the eternal God becomes Man. The One who would make known by his Cross the secret kept hidden through all ages is born of the Virgin Mary. So at this season "it is very meet, right and our bounden duty to give thanks unto thee, O Lord, Holy Father, Almighty, Everlasting God,

Because thou didst give Jesus Christ thine only Son to be born as at this time for us; who, by the operation of the Holy Ghost, was made very man of the substance of the Virgin Mary his mother; and that without spot of sin, to make us clean from sin.

We may speak of the mystery of the Incarnation, not only because it is beyond our understanding that God became Man but also because the Incarnation was for a purpose - the salvation of the world at the Cross. By the *mysterion* we are made "clean from sin."

The four Sundays of Advent (*adventus* = coming) exist to turn the thoughts and affections towards the Lord Jesus Christ in heaven who came into this world, "born of a woman and born under the law" (Gal.4:4) and who will return to this world "to judge the living and the dead." Only with a whole view of Christ and a full knowledge of Him, His identity and work, can there be true joy and gladness at Christmas. During Advent the faithful gain a sense of the *mystery* which is the summing up of all things in Christ at the end of the age when He comes to judge the living and the dead (Eph. 1:9-10).

Only when the festival is seen in the light of the kingdom of God of which He is the King can there be genuine celebration of the grace of God. For unless this festival is approached and experienced in the Spirit and with the light of biblical truth it can so easily be sentimentalized. In terms of knowing God the festival is a marvelous opportunity to contemplate "the weakness of God" as seen in the helpless baby's dependence upon Mary, His mother, and in the condescension of God not merely to our level but to our lowest level, in order to save us. "Thou shalt call his name Jesus for he will save his people from their sins" (Matt.1:21).

Other events described in the Gospels and specifically related to the birth of Jesus have been given dates in relation to Christmas Day. On March 25 is *The Annunciation of the Blessed Virgin Mary,* nine months before Christmas; on January 1 is *The Circumcision of Christ,* eight days after his birth and on February 2 is *The Presentation of Christ in the Temple,* according to Jewish law. Finally on June 24 is *The Nativity of John the Baptist,* who was born several months before Jesus.

Also related to Christmas and the Incarnation of the Son of God are the twelve days of Christmas which run from Christmas Day to Epiphany, "the Manifestation of Christ to the Gentiles". In terms of the *mysterion* the Epiphany is of great importance because an aspect of God's long-kept secret is, as Paul puts it, "that the Gentiles should be fellow-heirs, and of the same body [as the Jews] and partakers of his promise in Christ by the gospel" (Eph.3:7). The visit of the Gentile astrologers was a pointer in this direction.

Easter

In the period before, during, and after Easter the faithful are particularly conscious of the *mysterion.* For they are brought into vital contact with the Lord Christ who died for their sins, rose for their justification and ever lives to make intercession for them.

The date of Easter varies from year to year because it is fixed with respect to the Jewish Passover, and this, in turn, is based on the phases of the moon. Easter Day is always the Sunday after the full moon that occurs on or after the Spring equinox on March 21. Thus Easter cannot be any earlier than March 22 or later than April 25.

The two all-important days are Good Friday, the day of the crucifixion, and Easter Sunday, the day of the resurrection. Before Good Friday is Lent and Maundy Thursday and after Easter Day are the forty days to the Ascension and a further ten days to Whit-Sunday. One may think of the *mysterion* in relation to the whole period and one many also think of aspects of the *mysterion* in relation to specific days.

Casting our minds over the whole period we can see how there is the preparation through testing of Jesus for his final suffering and sacrificial death, and descent into hell. Here God is reconciling the world to Himself in His beloved Son in a way which defies all the wisdom of the world (1 Cor.1-2). *The mystery hidden in God is at last revealed for the salvation of the world.* By raising Jesus from the dead and exalting Him to His right hand in heaven, the Father almighty declares that there is a gospel for the world: the apostles have a *mystery* to proclaim to the whole world. By sending the Holy Spirit to unite His covenant people to His beloved Son, as his Body, the Father reveals another dimension to the *Mysterion*. The believers as the new covenant people of God are the Bride of Christ, united to Him by the Spirit in *mystical* union and in each person the same Spirit dwells, granting thereby *mystical* experience to him or her.

All these themes are to be found in the Collects, Epistles and Gospels for this period. For the believer this holy time provides a wonderful opportunity, in Paul's words, for the expression of this desire: "that I may know Christ, and the power of his resurrection and the fellowship of his sufferings, being made conformable unto his death" (Phil. 2:10).

Following the fifty days there begins the long season of Trinity, when the faithful have space and time to reflect upon and enjoy communion with the Father through the Son and by the Holy Spirit. The God who is Three in One and One in Three is Creator and Redeemer, Sustainer and Judge, Revealer and Provider, and many aspects of His relationship to mankind are brought before our attention in this period. The Collect for the last Sunday, the Twenty-Fifth, brings the Year to an end. It prays that religion, learned and experienced in church, will be the religion of daily life. In modern terms, liturgy is for life.

Stir up, we beseech thee, O Lord, the wills of thy faithful people; that they, plenteously bringing forth the fruit of good works, may of thee be plenteously rewarded; through Jesus Christ our Lord. Amen.

This is the last prayer on the lips before Advent Sunday arrives and the whole cycle of knowing God through the Church Year begins again.

Finally we need to remember the holy days on which New Testament saints, and All Saints, are remembered (often called red letter days because they were printed in red in old Prayer Books). They were faithful to the *mysterion* and in them it was reflected, the *mystery* of "Christ in you the hope of glory" (Col. 1:27).

10

COMMON PRAYER

A popular expression, much loved of those engaged in the study of liturgy is this—*lex orandi: lex credendi.* It is usually quoted in Latin, which sounds more imposing and awesome than the English translation, "the law of praying: the law of believing." (Technically it may also be translated "the law of believing: the law of praying.")

The Preface to the *BAS* (1985) of the Canadian Church clearly reveals that the architects of this book believed they were working according to this supposed hallowed principle. We read that,

It is precisely the intimate relationship of gospel, liturgy and service that stands behind the theological principle, lex orandi: lex credendi, i.e., the law of prayer is the law of belief. This principle, particularly treasured by Anglicans, means that theology as the statement of the Church's belief is drawn from the liturgy, i.e., from the point at which the gospel and the challenge of Christian life meet in prayer. The development of theology is not a legislative process which is imposed on liturgy; liturgy is a reflective process in which theology may be discovered. The Church must be open to liturgical change in order to maintain sensitivity to the impact of the gospel on the world and to permit the continuous development of a living theology.

This is a remarkable paragraph based as much on ignorance as prejudice. Similar statements both spoken and written abound and their abundance testifies to the move away from classic Anglicanism by those who, for the most part, now effectively order and run the worship of Anglicans. The same type of claims were made by those who created the *BCP* (1979), although at first they pretended that they were merely updating the Common Prayer Tradition and keeping its doctrinal framework.

Wrong way round?

First of all, the claim "it is precisely..." supposes that the writers have done careful historical research and can document their case. Such a possibility is doubtful. In fact if the Pope, and particularly Pope Pius XII, is any guide, then this expression is not a safe or sure guide. In his famous encyclical letter, *Mediator Dei* (1947), this Pope referred to the error and fallacious reasoning of those who claim that the sacred Liturgy is a kind of proving-ground for the truths to be held by faith. Such is not what the Church teaches and enjoins, he maintained. The entire Liturgy ought to have the Catholic Faith for its content, inasmuch as the Liturgy bears witness to the Faith of the Church.

He certainly recognized that on occasions the content of the Liturgy has been examined as one way (alongside others) of gaining insight into a controversial or doubtful truth. Yet the Pope concluded: "If one desires to differentiate and describe the relationship between Faith and the sacred Liturgy in absolute and general terms, it is perfectly correct to say: *Lex credendi legem statuat supplicandi* (let the rule of belief determine the rule of prayer)." This is precisely the opposite of the way *lex orandi: lex credendi* is used today.

In fact the origin of the expression, *lex orandi: lex credendi*, seems to have been with Prosper, a disciple of the great St Augustine of Hippo. He did not actually use it but another similar one which is the fore-runner of it: *lex supplicandi statuat legem credendi* (let the rule of prayer determine the rule of faith). Prosper was involved in a controversy [known as the Pelagian controversy] concerning the grace of God offered in Christ and the freedom of man to accept or reject it. Being a disciple of Augustine, he held that our wills are in a bondage to sin and until God releases them and gives them the freedom to choose Christ and to believe on His name then we are not able to do so. In order to show that this doctrine of God's sovereign grace was truly the faith of the Church, he appealed to the contents of the prayers offered by Christians. He believed that these assumed that without God we can do nothing for our salvation.

Therefore he could confidently say, in this specific context, that the rule of prayer tells us what is the rule of faith. Of course he and his master, Augustine, did not stop there; they also turned to the Scripture to study its message and to the Creeds of the Church to learn what they declared. In fact for the early fathers of the Church the *lex credendi* was to be found in the Holy Scriptures and to this the Liturgy was to witness and had to conform. If it conformed then it could be said in a strictly limited way that the law of prayer is the law of faith.—e.g. it confirmed Prosper's point that we are dependent upon God's grace in order to choose Christ. But such a law was not then, and cannot be now, of total or universal application in all circumstances.

Treasured by Anglicans?

Certainly since the sixteenth century, Anglicans have believed that in the *Book of Common Prayer* (in which historically were bound not only the Prayer Book proper but also the *Ordinal* and the *Thirty-Nine Articles*) is the *lex credendi*. For where you have the commitment to the authority of the Scriptures (the written Word of God), and a further commitment both to the catholic Creeds, and alongside the Creeds to the *Thirty-Nine Articles*, then you certainly have a *lex credendi*—which is more developed if you add the doctrines of the *Ordinal* concerning the Threefold Ministry. However, the *lex* is not primarily to be found in the whole Book but specifically in the doctrinal truth of the Scriptures and the dogma of the Creeds as summarizing the truth of Scripture. Thus to claim with the *BAS* (1985) that the *lex orandi: lex credendi* is a principle particularly treasured by Anglicans is true but only in a limited way. Further, it is true only of the Common Prayer Tradition in which the *BAS* (1985) hardly partakes.

The *BCP* (1549;1552;1662 etc.) was written from a theological, doctrinal and dogmatic perspective. It was held by Archbishop Cranmer and his colleagues that God expected the English Church to wash its dirty face in the sixteenth century with the "holy water" of the Gospel of Jesus Christ. For God had given to His Church the Two Testaments in the One Bible containing God's Word, together with the means to understand it through the holy Tradition of the first five or so centuries of the Catholic Church. Thus they spoke of five centuries, four general councils and two or three Creeds along with the development of doctrine and guidance in the interpretation of Scripture through important literature from the early fathers (e.g. Athanasius, Basil and Augustine). The *BCP* Liturgy was intended to express this Faith and thus be true to the Gospel of Jesus Christ. The fact that there have been continuing minor revisions of this Common Prayer Tradition over the centuries shows that no Liturgy as a collection of services can ever be a perfect embodiment of either the law of prayer or the law of belief. Yet this Common Prayer Tradition aims at excellence.

Liturgy, as written documents, reflects the beliefs of the writers even when they use or utilize ancient sources. Cranmer and his colleagues were vitally committed to the dogma of the early councils of the Church concerning God, the Holy Trinity, and Jesus Christ as God Incarnate, One Person with two natures, which they believed correctly summarized the basic testimony of Holy Scripture: thus these dogmas are clearly set forth in and through what they produced. But so also are other doctrinal aspects of the *lex credendi* which they wanted to make a part of the Liturgy. In particular it is obvious that the liturgy of the Lord's Supper is deeply informed both by the Augustinian doctrine of sin and the Augustinian doctrine of grace (as that is filtered through the emphasis of the Reformation on justification by faith). Much of course was received from the late medieval Church and adapted to fit into the new liturgical structures and renewed doctrinal framework to which the first *Books of Common Prayer* testify.

If asked, the English reformers would surely have claimed with Pius XII that it is perfectly correct to say, *lex credendi legem statuat supplicandi* (let the rule of belief determine the rule of prayer). In fact a careful reading of the *Thirty-Nine Articles* of Religion confirms this. Further, testimonies to the priority of the *lex credendi* abound in Anglican history. The judicious and learned Lancelot Andrewes wrote: "That which we learned *in lege credendi* [Apostles Creed] is taught again *in lege supplicandi* [meaning prayer which proceeds from the Lord's Prayer]" and went on to show that the law of praying is meant to establish and confirm the law of believing (*Sermons of the Lord's Prayer*, 1580, sermon vii).

The real difference between the modern creators of liturgies and their ancient predecessors is that for the latter, unlike the former, the principle of *sola scriptura*, the Scripture alone as the basis of faith, is non-negotiable and fundamental. Today's writers apparently see the Scriptures as one important but not the sole source of what we are to believe concerning God and our salvation. They allow to the world (through its *zeitgeist* or liberal culture) a certain illuminative role in establishing what we are to believe or what we may not believe. This is seen in their modern, revisionist translations of the ancient Creeds, their writing of new collects, their rubrical instructions and their inclusive language translations of the Bible. Thus while the services have the appearance of being genuinely Anglican and Catholic their inner substance represents so often a weakening or a changing of doctrine.

Not merely do liturgical experts produce modern services (that is in modern language) but they produce modern services containing modernity itself. This fact is often hidden from modern people because the experts often claim with some justification ancient pedigree for some of what they introduce. In fact a kind of archaeological interest seems to intrigue them and so anything from the fourth century or earlier has a special claim on their attention. Yet this kind of claim often conveniently hides behind the vague statements quoted above from the Preface of the *BAS* (1985). What does it mean to say that liturgy is a process in which theology may be discovered? Probably, that the longer the church uses the modern rites the more it will realize how much modernity is in them! And from the standpoint of the creators of the liturgy this will be a good thing for they are committed to what is often called "the modern experiment." Further, new liturgies will continue this experiment.

The great stability and value of the Common Prayer Tradition is its wholesome commitment to biblical and catholic truth as the basis of prayer and thus of knowing God. To move away from this norm is to move away from sure contact with the living God and His Revelation. Of course it is possible to have modern services which are faithful to Scripture and orthodox Christian dogma; regrettably so few modern liturgical experts seem to produce such liturgy.

Mix and Match

In the Common Prayer Tradition it is taken for granted that in public worship there will be a fixed form, with very few options and none in essentials. To find one's place is easy and to follow the service is straightforward. This stability and reliability stands in direct contrast to the modern form of liturgy which is fast becoming the provision of a loose-leaf book of resources from which each local church may select its own choice. Thus there is today the near triumph of mix-and-match and the demise of the principle and practice of common prayer. The name Anglican on the notice board can no longer guarantee for you or me a particular kind of Liturgy. Even if that church uses a printed Prayer Book and not a local collection from the loose-leaf resource book it still may offer you or me one of many possible combinations from there.

The Anglican Way as it developed in the Church of England from the sixteenth century and from England spread in all directions through the British Empire and missionary endeavors became a special (perhaps unique!) form and expression of the one, holy, catholic and apostolic church. It is biblical yet not biblicist; it is catholic yet evangelical; it is dignified but accessible to all regardless of social class or education. It is of such a nature that it can take within itself and benefit from a variety of churchmanships and different schools of spirituality and mission. Its special qualities make it just as appealing as the Liturgy of the Orthodox or Roman Catholic Churches and its genius is that it took in from the Protestant Reformation the biblical principle that all worship should conform to Scripture and contribute to the sanctification of those believers whom God justifies by His grace. For what Christ has done for us by His atoning death and glorious resurrection the Spirit wants to make real within our souls and bodies through the knowing of God in Common Prayer in all its forms.

Common Prayer is the whole collection of liturgies in the *BCP* and also it is the bond that unites them. In and through the use of them all, or such as apply to us at any one time, there is established a total rhythm of prayer which is based upon and always sustained by the Word of God. Persistent and mindless variations within Common Prayer cause this rhythm to be lost or its biblical basis overturned. There can be no regular mixing-and-matching for such a move destroys the rhythm with its logic of faith. For example, to use Morning Prayer as if the first part (the call to repentance and confession and the hearing of the Word of grace and forgiveness) did not really matter is to lose not only the principle of Common Prayer but also the biblical thread of salvation that informs it and holds it together. In technical terms (as Cranmer and Richard Hooker put it) Scripture as the doctrinal instrument of salvation lies at the very heart of the Common Prayer Tradition. Thus it is important to note that the printing of the Collect, Epistle and Gospel for each Sunday of the Year as well as for each Holy Day makes them an integral part of this Tradition. So the place of Scripture in determining the nature and path of public prayer is clearly recognized and followed. And around this center there is the reading and praying of the psalter once a month and the reading through of the whole Bible once a year (with parts of the New Testament read more than once) in the Daily Office.

The Common Prayer also speaks to community, and fellowship for worship is offered in Christ's name to the Father in the Holy Spirit by the Body of Christ. Regrettably, the Common Prayer Tradition has been made into something less than the experience of unity in Christ in worship. This is usually attributed to the dominance in days of old of Matins as the major service of the Lord's Day; but, it is more to be blamed on insufficient teaching of what our common life together in the Lord Jesus is all about. Where there is the pattern of the Daily Office along with Holy Communion on the Lord's Day and where there is teaching from the Scriptures which are being continuously read in the Daily Office, then the Common Prayer will also begin to be common fellowship. For there is no doubt that the Scriptures which lie at the very center of the Anglican Way do call for and expect God's people to be truly a fellowship of believers: they are to know God in prayer and know God through each other in fellowship.

Unlike modern liturgies which deliberately aim to use popular, forgettable and low-key language, the Common Prayer Tradition has excellency as its aim. Thus each service is presented in excellent English so that all can (perhaps with effort and some instruction) understand it. As they understand it they will be uplifted by the experience of participating in it and, further, in regularly using it they will not be bored by it but rather its very excellency will enable them to say it often and gain in the using of it. The fact that the

English of the Common Prayer Tradition is not now spoken is no argument against using it. Experience shows that it can be easily understood and is an excellent means of magnifying the name of the Lord our God. In fact for a congregation to use it in sincerity and truth adds to the genuine experience of fellowship in that society of Christians. It is also interesting but not surprising for me to learn that university students in England who sing or say Daily Prayer in the College chapels prefer the *BCP* (1662) to the *ASB* (1980). Their reason is simply that the excellency of the liturgy of *BCP* (1662) helps them more quickly and easily to enter into the ethos of worship. In the house of the Lord surely we ought to praise our God from the heart in the finest and most excellent words which express our faith..

In the *BCP* tradition "common" refers to that which belongs to all and is accessible by and to all. It is for all to use together. Therefore all, without exception, who attend the parish church services use the identical forms of worship all the time. Thus they need to be in excellent form and language. Today "common" in the title of the American *BCP* (1979) hardly means what it meant in the *BCP* (1928) for the intention of the former Book is to set up a new model of prayer—that of variety and mixing-and-matching, so that there is something for everyone (or at least for every priest or worship committee who do the choosing). It is inclusive in that provision is made in it for people of all kinds to participate in the modern styles of worship. Again we readily admit that where wise people do the choosing a good service of worship can result.

This difference in the meaning of "common" is easily illustrated by looking at the services in the two American Books for visiting the sick. The traditional rite in *BCP* (1928) precedes the sacramental actions of anointing, absolution and holy communion with Psalms and prayers offered for and with the sick person. The revised rite in *BCP* (1979) introduces these sacramental actions with a reading of Bible lessons to the sick. The model for the revised rite is taken from the Sunday Eucharist so that the Psalm is read as a gradual between the Epistle and the Gospel. The model for the old rite is the Daily Office with its basic structure of Psalms and prayers. In the old rite it was assumed that the sick person could join in the familiar Psalms and prayers either vocally or in his heart for they represented the common prayer of the Church offered daily to the Lord. In the new rite it is assumed that common prayer does not exist and that the only form people will know or be used to is that of the Sunday Eucharist. There is no doubt in my mind which of these models is superior at the pastoral level!

In their expositions of the Common Prayer Tradition many Anglicans from Cranmer to C.S.Lewis have made the point that there is great spiritual value when worshippers are able to give themselves wholly to their high calling because they are using week by week the same, near-perfect expressions for praise and petition. They know always what is coming next and so are not unnecessarily shaken in their concentration upon the act of worship. Writing three centuries ago William Beveridge, Bishop of St Asaph, explained the difference from the point of view of the worshppers between set prayer and *ex temporare* prayer. What he wrote also applies to modern mix-and-match liturgy:

> Moreover, that which conduceth to the quickening our souls and to the raising of our affections must needs be acknowledged to conduce much to edification. But it is plain that for such purposes a set form of prayer is an extraordinary help to us. For, if I hear another pray and know not beforehand what he will say, I must first listen to what he will say next: then I am to consider whether what he saith be agreeable to sound doctrine, and whether it be proper and lawful for me to join with him in the petitions he puts up to God Almighty: and if I think it is so, then I am to do it. But before I can well do that, he is got to another thing; by which means it is very difficult, if not morally impossible, to join

with him in everything so regularly as I ought to do. But by a set form of prayer all this trouble is prevented; for having the form continually in my mind, being thoroughly acquainted with it, fully approving of everything in it, and always knowing beforehand what will come next, I have nothing else to do, whilst the words are sounding in mine ears, but to move my heart and affections suitably to them, to raise up my desires of those good things which are prayed for, to fix my mind wholly upon God whilst I am praising of him, and so to employ, quicken and lift up my soul in performing my devotions to him. No man that hath been accustomed to a set form for any considerable time, but may easily find this to be true by his own experience, and, by consequence, that this way of praying is a greater help to us than they can imagine that never made trial of it (*A Sermon on the Excellency of the Common Prayer*,1681).

These are wise words and had priests given explanations like this to young people then there would have been a greater understanding and deeper commitment to the Common Prayer Tradition in the 1960s and 1970s and the story of liturgical revision would probably have been a very different one than it has been. Divine service is not the place for experiment or for leaders to share their latest liturgical fads and fancies. It is the meeting with Almighty God, who calls us into His presence as His covenant people in the name of the Lord Jesus Christ. To gain fully from this encounter we need the most excellent form of words available to us.

Wisdom from Bishop Hobart

[In his *Companion to the Festivals and Fasts* (1804) Bishop Hobart had the following explanations of Common Prayer.]

Q. Since our Church has prescribed a form of prayer or Liturgy, for the public service of the Church, state some of the particular advantages of forms of prayer.

A. When a form of prayer is used, the people are previously acquainted with the prayers in which they are to join, and are thus enabled to render unto God a reasonable and enlightened service. In forms of prayer, the greatest dignity and propriety of sentiment may be secured. They prevent the particular opinions and dispositions of the minister from influencing the devotions of the congregation; they serve as a standard of faith and practice; and they render the service more animating, by uniting the people with the minister in the performance of public worship.

Q. What are the peculiar excellences of the Liturgy prescribed by our Church?

A. In the Liturgy of our Church there is an admirable mixture of instruction and devotion. The Lessons, the Creeds, the Commandments, the Epistles and Gospels, contain the most important and impressive instruction on the doctrines and duties of religion; while the Confession, the Collects and Prayers, the Litany and Thanksgivings, lead the understanding and the heart through all the sublime and affecting exercises of devotion. In this truly evangelical and excellent Liturgy, the supreme Lord of the universe is invoked by the most appropriate, affecting and sublime epithets; all the wants to which man, as a dependent and sinful being, is subject, are expressed in language at once simple, concise, and comprehensive; these wants are urged by confessions the most humble, and supplications the most reverential and ardent; the all-sufficient merits of Jesus Christ, the Saviour of the world, are uniformly urged as the only effectual plea, the only certain pledge of divine mercy and grace; and with the most instructive lessons from the sacred oracles, and the most profound confessions and supplications, is mingled the sublime chorus of praise, begun by the minister, and responded with one heart and voice from the assembled congregation.

The mind, continually passing from one exercise of worship to another, and, instead of one continued and uniform prayer, sending up its wishes and aspirations in short and varied collects and supplications, is never suffered to grow languid or weary. The affections of the worshipper ever kept alive by the tender and animating fervour which breathes through the service, he worships his God and Redeemer in spirit and in truth, with reverence and awe, with lively gratitude and love; the exalted joys of devotion are poured upon his soul; he feels that it is good for him to draw near unto God, and that a day spent in his courts is better than a thousand passed in the tents of the ungodly.

11

LANGUAGE FOR GOD

The Common Prayer Tradition assumes that God has named and described Himself and thus in addressing Him in prayer His worshippers are to keep to these names and descriptions. (At the end of this chapter a list of these names and titles is provided.) In this assumption there is a basic commitment to the authority of Scripture, but there is a recognition that a national Church does have liberty within the biblical range of names and descriptions to use some more than others. In terms of names those of the three Persons of the most Holy Trinity do, of course, along with such names as "Lord" and "King", have pride of place and in terms of descriptions, words such as "Almighty" and "Everlasting" are used often.

Inclusive Language

If this is the case why has there been so much talk within liberal denominations, including the Episcopal Church, of the need for inclusive language, not only for speaking of human beings but also for the naming and addressing of their Creator and Redeemer? Why do we hear of bishops giving the Blessing in "the name of God, Creator, Redeemer and Sanctifier", and refusing to use the names of "the Father and the Son and the Holy Spirit?" Why do some modern forms of service begin the Lord's Prayer with "Our Father-Mother..." instead of just "our Father...?" Why is the referring to the Holy Spirit as "She" becoming so common? And why is there in some quarters the prohibition of the name "Lord" for Jesus or for God?

The answer to all these questions is very simple - the authority of the Holy Scripture, the Creeds and of traditional theology has waned and the authority and power of modern secular thinking and culture have risen. The wind of feminism, anti-sexism and anti-patriarchy has blown through the churches and since their windows were wide open to it they have felt its force. The clergy in particular have developed a sense of guilt about their addressing of God in exclusively male terms and to show that they truly believe in the equality of women they have been ready to adopt female names for God such as "mother" to try to bring in fair-play as they see it. For the majority who have adopted inclusivism there have been no theological considerations: they have simply thought that they had to move with the times and show that they really believed in the equality of men and women in the Church. Thus hand in hand with the ordaining of women as priests has gone an increasing commitment to inclusive language for God.

Therefore it is not surprising that the emphasis on equality for women in terms of entry to the ordained ministry seems to require a change in both the doctrine and the forms of worship of the churches today. This is because the activists for equal rights and feminism are not satisfied with anything less than a total change in the way that congregations address God and ministers name God in public services and in official documents and reports.

Certainly it is usually the case that for the leaders of these causes the call for the changing of the names of God is based on a view or doctrine of God. In chapter three we discussed theism, deism, panentheism and pantheism and emphasized that Christianity is committed to Trinitarian Theism. Those who have been and still are pressing for changes in the naming and addressing of God are usually committed to deism or panentheism or pantheism. In contrast those who insist that the churches are already committed, and ought to stay committed, to the revealed names of God in Scripture are invariably Trinitarian Theists. For to be Trinitarian is to confess that God has not only revealed that

He is Three Persons but that each Person has a name which comes out of the self-naming of God by God Himself.

It is important to recognize that according to the Bible God chooses to be known through and by His names. Thus in terms of the knowing and having communion with God it is of supreme importance that His creatures name Him in ways that are pleasing to Him. The primary confession of the Christian is "Jesus is Lord" and it is in the naming of Jesus as Lord (Rom. 10:9; Phil. 2:11) and thus in the giving to him of the worship and obedience contained in that name that the believer both knows Jesus and is known by him.

Jesus himself, the eternal Son made Man (that is the Man for others), addressed God in heaven in a very particular way. Over and over again we read of him in all the Gospels both speaking of and addressing God in heaven as "Father". His moving, priestly prayer in John 17 contains several addresses "O Father" and one "O righteous Father." Then when asked by his disciples how they ought to pray he taught them to begin, "Our Father, which art in heaven, hallowed be thy Name..." Continuing this way of prayer we find that St Paul speaks often of "the God and Father of our Lord Jesus Christ" (2 Cor.1:2-3) and himself prays to the Father, through the Son and in the Holy Spirit (Rom.8). And this is the basic pattern of the prayers of the early Church and of the Common Prayer Tradition. We address the FATHER through the SON in the HOLY SPIRIT.

It seems to me that Dr James I Packer, the leading Anglican Evangelical theologian, put this matter very clearly when he wrote:

> You sum up the whole of New Testament teaching in a single phrase, if you speak of it as a revelation of the Fatherhood of the holy Creator. In the same way, you sum up the whole of New Testament religion if you describe it as the knowledge of God as one's holy Father. If you want to judge how well a person understands Christianity, find out how

much he makes of the thought of being God's child, and having God as his Father. If this is not the thought that prompts and controls his worship and prayers and his whole outlook on life, it means that he does not understand Christianity very well at all. For everything that Christ taught, everything that makes the New Testament new, and better than the Old, everything that is distinctively Christian as opposed to merely Jewish, is summed up in the knowledge of the Fatherhood of God. "Father" is the Christian name for God (*Evangelical Magazine*, vol.7, p.19).

If Packer is right, and I believe that he is, then those who want to minimize or set aside the name "Father" do not "understand Christianity very well at all."

Arguments offered

Those who want to set aside this biblical way of prayer and of knowing God as the Triune LORD use a variety of devices. One is to claim that there is within the Bible a suppressed tradition of understanding, devotion and prayer which uses female images and names for God. Certainly there are a few similes in the Old and New Testaments which compare the gracious character of God to that of a loving mother bird or human mother who cares for her offspring (see e.g. Is. 66:13; Matt.23:37). Then because the grammatical gender of "wisdom" in Hebrew is female it is alleged that since God's wisdom is personified (e.g. Prov.8) then God may rightly be called "She" and we may use feminine pronouns of the deity. Of course orthodox Christianity should speak of God's mercy through the use of similes drawn from the love of mothers; however, it cannot jump from the recognition of grammatical gender to a doctrinal claim! And to say God is like a mother is not the same as saying "O God, our mother." A simile is not a title!

Another argument follows from the claim that God is utter Mystery, that he is totally beyond our comprehension and understanding. This being so, it is claimed, no words, not even Bible names, can be sufficient in and of themselves to evoke in us the truth and sense of God as Mystery. In fact, the names used by the Bible and in the early Church were probably socially conditioned and thus reflect the patriarchal, androcentric culture of those times. So in naming the Mystery we are free to use those names and expressions for God which flow from our experience and cultural roots and seem authentic to and for us. Since our culture is moving away from the dominance of men to the practice of equality of men and women, it is said that we ought to reflect this move in our naming and addressing of God and be bold to call God "Mother" and "Sister", or use verbal nouns such as "cosmic Regenerator" and "ineffable Sanctifier."

This kind of argument has to be challenged on two fronts. First, one admits that there is in the Church a tradition of theology which recognizes that God is Mystery (better, the Mystery) for He is supremely above all our knowledge and experience. We recognize this in theology by speaking of the *Via Negativa,* the way of saying who God is by saying what He is not. This method does not seek to describe or name God but it certainly makes clear that God is other than everything we think of and know in this finite world. God is Mystery for we do not know His Being—all we can say is that He is super-essential Being. However, and secondly, alongside the *Via Negativa,* has always stood the *Via Affirmativa,* the way of affirming who God is—not out of human knowledge—but from God's self-unveiling in His Revelation through the prophets and uniquely in Jesus Christ. It is only because of this Revelation that the Church dares to name God for she learns that God has already self-named Himself. The Church names God in fear and trembling by His own names, recognizing that who He is to her is contained in these names. These are the name of His covenant relationship with His new Israel. He who revealed His name as LORD [Yahweh, Jehovah] to Moses and the old

Israel revealed His name to the new Israel as the LORD, who is the Father, the Son and the Holy Spirit.

A third argument, and one which can be very influential at the personal and parochial level, is psychological. It usually comes from persons who have had a bad relationship with a man, either a father, brother or husband. Your hear a very sincere woman say something like this: "It was so liberating to learn that I can call God 'Mother' and think of God in feminine ways," and usually her story is of being abused by her father. In order to be healed she needs, not to name God as "She" and "Mother" as she has been led to believe, but to sort out her feelings and thoughts concerning her father and men in general. When she has achieved psychological health then she can address theological problems.

Then there are women who constantly claim that they are abused or belittled by traditional Christian worship for their equality with men before God is denied if God is only addressed in worship in male terms—Father, Son, Lord, King, and Bridegroom—and thus the worship assumes that patriarchy is not only true but also is God's will. It is difficult to know whether these women really are expressing deep hurt as such or whether they are expressing an ideology of feminism through the medium of claimed hurt feelings. How one seeks to minister to them will depend upon where they are coming from in these assertions and claims of hurt.

Defending biblical language

I have come to the conclusion after writing a book (*Let God be God*, 1990) and giving many talks on the topic, "Inclusive language, right or wrong?", that the only way to defend traditional biblical language for God is to argue for it from the primary doctrine of divine order.

First of all, however, I need to address those who are pushing for inclusive language their doctrine of God. Usually I find that those who are loudest and most zealous for renaming God are not theists and thus have no rightful claim to be seeking to change the names of the God whom Christians have explained in theistic terms. Usually they have a concept of God which includes the world within the being of God. That is, if the world were taken out of their concept of God there would be only one part or dimension or aspect of God left! (Such a view stands of course in complete contrast to classical Christian theism where God minus the world equals God.)

It is often said today in seminaries and religious conferences that the world is in God but that God, since he/she includes the world in his/her being, is more than the world. Or that God and the world (which may or may not be within God) are in mutual attraction and development, each being changed by the other as day succeeds day. This panentheism or process theology easily marries with earth-mother and mother-goddess talk. In fact if the world is in God and if God is developing in and through the world, then in the bringing forth of new life each Spring God is like a mother - so God may be called and addressed as a mother.

I also find that this way of thinking of the world as being within the being of God with the world and God mutually affecting each other as they develop together is often married to aspects of Jungian (depths) psychology. For example, I heard a sermon at an Anglican Conference recently based upon the text, "Unless you become as little children..." (Matt.18:2-3), in which a woman explained that there is in each of us a divine child waiting to be born and to develop in and through us; and further that God as the divine Mother is there waiting and ready to bring this child to birth within and through us. Here I heard both Jungian psychology and panentheism.

So unless I can persuade those who hold such views to turn from them to classical Christian theism there is little hope of their seeing the necessity of only using such names as are permitted by God Himself.

The belief and the doctrine that God has named God begins with confession of faith in the Holy Trinity. God as the LORD transcends and is beyond all sexuality: God as God does not have either a male or female nature for God as God has a divine nature. Within the One Godhead of the Three Persons there is both perfect equality (for all share the One Godhead) and an ordered relation. The First Person, who is self-named the Father, eternally begets the Son before all ages; the Son, who is named by the Father, is therefore in a particular relation, Sonship, to the Father; the Holy Spirit, who is named by the Father eternally proceeds from the Father through the Son. Here there is perfect equality but ordered relation within the One Godhead. Here there is also the naming of the three Persons by the First Person (with the agreement of the Second and Third Persons) in order for the angels and archangels as well as earthly creatures to address and adore their LORD, a Trinity in Unity.

The One God in whom is an ordered relation of Three Persons is the Creator of the world. The Father speaks His creating and sustaining Word as and through the Son in the power of the Holy Spirit. Thus the invisible world of arch-angels and angels, cherubim and seraphim comes to be and the visible world in which we live, and move and have our being also comes to be. In each case there is an ordered relation, first to God, the Creator and Judge, and second of parts of the creation to other parts of the same creation. In terms of human beings God created male and female human beings, who are truly equal before Him in terms of their being made in His image and after His likeness, in an ordered relation. The woman is not the man and the man is not the woman but their relation is of the priority of the man. This is set forth in the Genesis narrative through the story of the woman being made from the man's rib (Gen.2:22-23). St Paul teaches this with clarity especially in his First Letter to Corinth, the Letter to Ephesus and the Letters to Timothy.

Only in this kind of context can we speak positively of patriarchy. If we take patriarchy to mean the ordered relation of men and women in which the man assumes his God-given place and vocation then we may say that patriarchy is biblical and reflects the hierarchical relations of the Blessed Trinity. Such patriarchy assumes therefore the perfect equality of man and woman in their differences and also establishes their relation in terms of hierarchy of order. To present this as God's design is not of course to claim that such order has existed except for brief periods here and there. We also have to tell the story of sin and how this has brought disease and rebellion against God and His holy order into all human souls and all relationships between husbands and wives, males and females, and men with men and women with women.

In this context of divine order we have a sound basis upon which to reject not only inclusive language for God but also much of the modern clamor for inclusive language for human beings. If we are Trinitarian Theists, if we believe that God has graciously revealed Himself to us in ways that we can understand (through the illumination of the Spirit) and if we believe that God has self-named God then our solemn and joyous duty is to ascertain God's names and use them in the way which is pleasing to Him. (To do this is, I believe, to walk in the way of the Common Prayer Tradition.) Further, if we believe that God is the God of Order, that God as God is an ordered, hierarchical relation of Persons in one Godhead, and that God has built ordered relations into His creation of the invisible and visible worlds, then our solemn and joyous duty is to submit to this order and use language which reflects it.

To use language which reflects it will include the readiness to use what is technically called generic language. The New Testament is written in this language and one of the purposes of new translations like the *New Standard Revised Version* is to set aside this language. Thus the Greek, *ad-*

elphoi, which literally means "brothers" is translated "brothers and sisters." In generic Greek or English "brethren" means both "brothers and sisters." In the Psalms the Hebrew noun, *ish,* meaning "the man" is translated as "they" (a third person neuter plural, in order to seek to cover male and female persons). In generic Hebrew and English "the man" includes his wife and family.

Together with this argument from divine order there is of course the historical fact that the Hebrew does actually say "the man" and not "they" and the Greek says "brethren" not "brothers and sisters." So there is a matter of honesty in translating ancient texts into English at stake as well. The *NRSV,* however, unlike the Psalter in the *BCP* (1979), does clearly indicate by footnotes most places where inclusivism has intruded into the translation.

But what about language for male and female persons in Liturgy? The Common Prayer Tradition uses generic language and in so doing reflected the use of language in the sixteenth and seventeenth centuries; but that usage accorded with the doctrine of divine order. Today the way of modern culture is to insist on inclusive language in the media, in education and most if not all areas of modern life. The Church, however, which is called not to be conformed to the world but to be transformed by being renewed in and after the mind of Christ, ought not to feel obliged to leave its generic language but to use it as a way of expressing divine order. Of course, in so doing, the Church would have to set aside the ordination of women as presbyters/priests and bishops because they do not fit into God's plans for His divine order.

Knowing God in Liturgy involves naming, addressing, adoring, praising and thanking Him according to His design and not after our sinful desires and ideas. If we draw near to Him in the way He has prescribed for us, then, as St James declares, He will draw near to us (Jas 4:8).

Advice from Bishop Hobart

[This excerpt comes from his *Companion for the BCP*]

It is much to be lamented, that the *POSTURE of KNEELING*, during the public prayers, is very generally neglected. In many churches, the boards provided for the purpose of kneeling, are used only as foot boards. The general prevalence of the posture of sitting during the solemn acts of confession and supplication must be a subject of deep regret with all who esteem the *decent* and *devout* performance of public worship a matter of the first importance. The late excellent and exemplary Bishop of London, Dr. Porteus, in a letter which he addressed in May 1804 to the clergy of his Diocese, thus enforces the duty of kneeling during the performance of prayer: "For many years past, I have observed with extreme concern, in different churches and chapels, both in the metropolis and in various parts of the country where I happened to be present, a practice prevailing (and evidently gaining ground every day) of a *considerable part of the congregation sitting during those parts of divine worship where the rubric expressly enjoins every one to kneel.*

"It may be thought, perhaps, that the posture of body in offering up our prayers, is a circumstance too trivial to deserve such serious notice as this. But can anything be trivial that relates to the Almighty Governor of the universe? Does not every one know, too, that the mind and the body mutually act upon and influence each other; and that a negligent attitude of the one will naturally produce indifference and inattention in the other? Look only at the general deportment of those who sit at their devotions (without being compelled to it by necessity), and then say whether this remark is not founded in truth and in fact. I shall be told, perhaps, that there are some denominations of Christians that *stand*, and others that *sit* at their devotions. It is very true, and they must be left to judge for themselves; but my concern at present is with members of the church. Our

Church, in her admirable form of public prayer, allows, in different parts of the service, the different postures both of standing and sitting; which, with her usual wisdom and discretion, she adapts to the respective circumstances of those particular parts. But where the solemnity and importance of our supplications require it, there she positively enjoins the posture of kneeling; and to disobey that injunction is unquestionably an offence against the discipline and usage of that venerable Church to which we have the happiness to belong.

"It is also contrary to the practice of the best, and greatest, and wisest men, both before the promulgation of the Gospel and after it. The exhortation of king *David* in the 95th Psalm, which we have adopted into our Liturgy, is, 'O come, let us worship, and fall down, and *kneel* before the LORD our Maker.' When *Solomon* dedicated his magnificent temple to God, he *kneeled* down upon his knees before all the congregation of Israel, and spread forth his hands towards heaven, while he poured forth one of the most sublime and affecting prayers that ever fell from the lips of man. It was the custom of the prophet *Daniel* to *kneel* upon his knees three times a day, and pray and give thanks unto his God. Our Saviour himself, in his last agony, *kneeled* down and prayed; *St. Stephen*, in his last moments, *kneeled down* and prayed for his murderers; and *St. Paul*, when he took his last solemn leave of his brethren, *kneeled* down even on the seashore, and offered up his petitions to heaven for their everlasting welfare.

"After these injunctions of the Church, and these examples from Scripture, no one, I think, who calls himself a Christian, and a member of the Church, will (unless prevented by *illness* or *infirmity*) refuse to *kneel down* before the Lord his Maker. But if you perceive any part of your congregation habitually neglecting so to do, I must request you to represent to them, in forcible terms, the great impropriety and indecency of such a practice. It is very possible that they may have fallen into it from mere thoughtlessness and inattention, and considered it as a matter of very little importance; but you will, I hope, endeavour to convince them that it is in reality a very serious offense against the Majesty of Heaven and the decorum and solemnity of public worship. It is evidently inconsistent with that profound reverence which is due to the great Creator of the universe, and that deep humility, and contrition which become such wretched sinners as we all are, in a greater or less degree, in the sight of God. It strikes, in short, in my apprehension, at the very root of all true devotion; and ought therefor to be vigorously resisted before it has gained too much strength to be subdued. If it is not, if it is suffered to go on without control, there is too much reason to apprehend, from the progress it has made within these few years, that it will in a few years more become a universal practice, and that you will see the whole of your congregation sitting during every part of divine service."

Addressing God in the Common Prayer Tradition

[In his fascinating book, *The Liturgy compared with the Bible,* Henry I Bailey provided a list of the "Epithets, Titles and Characters by which the Divine Being is addressed..." The list is given below along with a further list of expressions by which Almighty God is addressed.]

Epithets, Titles and Characters

Aid of all that need	Author of everlasting life
Author and giver of all good things	Author of peace
Comforter	Sovereign Commander of all the world
Head Corner-stone	Creator and Preserver of all mankind
Faithful Creator	Defender and Mighty Deliverer

Father of all mercies	Father of our Lord Jesus Christ
Father of heaven	Father of spirits
Almighty Father	God the Father Almighty
Heavenly Father	Most merciful Father
Fountain of all goodness	Fountain of all wisdom
Giver of all goodness	Giver of all good things
Giver of all spiritual grace	God the Father, God the Son, and God the Holy Ghost
God Almighty	God of Abraham, and of Isaac and of Jacob
God of all comfort	God of all mercy
God, just and powerful	God most mighty
God of God,	Almighty God
Almighty and everlasting God	Almighty and everliving God
Almighty and immortal God	Almighty and merciful God
Almighty and most merciful God and Saviour	Blessed Lord
Eternal God	Great God
Lord God of hosts	Lord our God
Lord God of our salvation	Lord God most holy
A merciful God	Most gracious God
Most mighty, gracious and good God	Most glorious and gracious Lord God
Most powerful and glorious Lord God	Perfect God

Very God of very God	Governor of all things
Only Help in time of need	Helper of them that flee to Him for succour
Most High	Judge of all men
Righteous Judge	Most worthy Judge eternal
Jesus	Jesus Christ
Blessed Jesus	Lord Jesus Christ
Only-begotten Son, Jesus Christ	King of glory
King of kings	Lamb of God
Immaculate Lamb	Life of them that believe
Light of Light	Lord
Lord of hosts	Lord of lords
Lord of all power and might	Lord most mighty
Lord and Giver of life	Lord in whose sight the death of his saints is precious
Blessed Lord	Lover of Concord
Divine Majesty	Maker of all things
Maker of heaven and earth	Maker of mankind
Our Master	Preserver of all mankind
Prince of Peace	Protector of all that trust in Him
Most Mighty Protector	Redeemer of the world
Refuge and Strength	Resurrection of the dead
Resurrection and the Life	Ruler of princes
Saviour	Saviour of the world

Saviour Christ	Blessed Saviour
Holy and most merciful Saviour	Shepherd
Son of David	Spirit of Christ
Blessed Spirit	Good Spirit
Holy Spirit	Strength of all them that put their trust in Him

Strong Tower of Defence

God is addressed, as

God, who desireth not the death of a sinner

God, who from his throne beholdeth all the dwellers upon earth

God, who despiseth not the sighing of a contrite heart

God, who alone worketh great marvels

God, who governeth all things in heaven and earth

God, who hateth nothing that He has made

God, who declareth His almighty power most chiefly in shewing mercy and pity

God, who of his infinite goodness hath given His only and dearly beloved Son to be our Redeemer and the Author of everlasting life

God, who by His Divine Providence hath appointed divers Orders of Ministers in His Church

God, who by His Holy Spirit hath appointed divers Orders of Ministers in His Church

God, who knoweth our necessities before we ask, and our ignorance in asking

God, who maketh us both to will and to do those things that be good and acceptable unto His Divine Majesty

God, who doth so put away the sins of those who truly repent that He remembereth them no more

God, who doth correct those whom he loveth, and chastiseth every one whom He doth receive

God, who hath compassion upon all men, and hateth nothing that He hath made

God, who alone spreadeth out the heavens, and ruleth the raging of the sea

God, who is of infinite goodness and mercy

God, whose mercy is over all His works

God, in whose hand is power and might, which none is able to withstand

God, whose name is excellent in all the earth, and His glory above the heavens

God, who is terrible in His judgements, and wonderful in His doings toward the children of men

God, who by His wisdom guideth and ordereth all things most suitably to His own justice

God, whose righteousness is like the strong mountains, and His judgements like the great deep

God, who ruleth over all the kingdoms of the world, and disposeth of them

God, who upholdeth and governeth all things in heaven and in earth

12

GOD IS LOVE

Christians do not confess that love is God; they confess that God, as the Almighty LORD, is Love. In fact the early Christians took a Greek word, *agape*, and made it their special word for speaking of the love that is in God, the love that causes God to reach out to save sinful creatures and the love which in saving them He places in their souls. Truly happy are those who know and feel that their God is Love.

Biblical reflection

The Epistle for the first Sunday after Trinity-Sunday is 1 John 4:7-21. Twice in this passage we hear one of the briefest but most important statements of the whole Bible: *God is love.* John wrote: "He that loveth not knoweth not God: for God is love. In this was manifested the love of God towards us, because that God sent His only begotten Son into the world, that we might live through Him. Herein is love, not that we loved God, but that He loved us, and sent his Son to be the propitiation for our sins."

To believe and confess that God is Love in the manner and spirit of St John is to sum up in three words what we learn about the one, living God from the whole of His self-revelation recorded in Holy Scripture. That is, to state that the LORD is Love is not to deny what is said in both the OT and NT of His wrath against sin and evil and of His chastising of His covenant people when they forsook Him and worshipped idols. Further, to say that God is Love is to say that the almighty God who made the whole universe out of nothing and maintains it moment by moment, He is Love. To affirm that God is Love is to say that the God who guided the patriarchs into Egypt and allowed their descendants to become slaves, He is love. Also to confess that God is Love is to say that the God who sent the tribes of Israel from Palestine into captivity and exile in Assyria and Babylon where many perished, He is Love. Further to confess that there is a hell and that God will send there those who totally reject His grace is to claim that such a God, He is Love. Finally to state that God is Love is to say that the God who caused the Messiah, Jesus of Nazareth, to suffer, to be crucified and to descend into hell, He is Love.

The God who is Love is the God of justice and righteousness. Anyone who tries to drive a wedge between the wrath and the love of God is not being instructed by the Holy Scriptures in his thinking. The God who punishes the disobedient is truly the God who is Love. This biblical approach to the character of God is a problem for us if we think or feel (as so many seem to do) that all love is God, rather than beginning with God and confessing with St John that God Himself is Love. Perhaps great harm has been done in the Church in recent times by seeking to describe God in terms of what is considered to be love amongst and in human beings. Certainly the Common Prayer Tradition is very clear on this point and directs worshippers always to God Himself for an understanding of what is genuine love, compassion, mercy and grace.

It is very important for us to grasp this point because the fact that God Himself is Love is the basis of the divine command that we love God and one another. In the Epistle for the first Sunday after Trinity-Sunday the second occurrence of "God is love" is as follows: "God is love; and he that dwelleth in love dwelleth in God and God in him...We love Him because he first loved us...he who loveth God loves his brother also." Therefore, it is extremely important that we know God and in knowing God know Him as Love in order that from and in that Love we are able to love our fellow men, especially our fellow believers in Christ.

Such is the prayer that Anglicans have offered to God on the Sunday immediately before Lent (Quinquagesima):

O LORD, who hast taught us that all our doings without charity [love] are nothing worth; send thy Holy Ghost, and pour into our hearts that most excellent gift of charity, the very bond of peace and all virtues, without which whosoever liveth is counted dead before thee: Grant this for thine only Son Jesus Christ's sake. Amen.

Following this Collect the Epistle is the great hymn of love written by Paul in 1 Corinthians 13. "Though I speak with the tongues of men and of angels, and have not charity [love], I am become as sounding brass, or a tinkling cymbal."

I think it is important that we notice that before John wrote "God is love" he wrote "God is light". He said: "This is the message which we declare unto you, that God is light, and in him is no darkness at all" (1:5). On this basis John proceeded to call upon his readers to "walk in the light as God is in the light" and thereby to have fellowship one with another and to experience the power of the forgiving, cleansing blood of Jesus Christ in their hearts and fellowship. Not to walk in the light (that is being enlightened and illumined by God's self-revelation and presence) is to walk in darkness (enlightened and illumined by the ethos and standards of this sinful world).

Bearing this in mind we have to say that "God is love" means "God is holy love" and "God is righteous love." God as love is not love divorced from absolute purity and righteousness: rather, His love is pure, holy and righteous love. God's love will, therefore, chastise and punish for God is not in the business of making people happy who will not seek for holiness and purity of life. However, to confess that "God is love" and "God is light" is to believe that in everything (with no exceptions) that God says and does His love and holiness find expression. To know God as the LORD is to know that God is entirely consistent in His character and His dealings with us: it is also to understand that we know what love really is from contemplating God rather than examining human actions and feelings.

There are some marvelous descriptions of the love of God in the writings of Paul apart from 1 Corinthians 13 cited above. In Romans 5 and 8 the apostle waxes eloquent concerning the presence of the love of God in the human soul: "the love of God is shed abroad in our hearts by the Holy Ghost which is given unto us" (5:5). Then he asks the rhetorical question: "Who shall separate us from the love of Christ?" (8:35) and comes quickly and eloquently to the conclusion that nothing whatsoever in the whole invisible or visible created worlds "shall be able to separate us from the love of God which is in Christ Jesus our Lord." Love, pure love, which is of God begins within the Godhead and is the essence of the relation of the Father to the Son and the Son to the Father, the relation of the Father to the Spirit and the Spirit to the Father, and the relation of the Son and the Spirit to each other. God is Love as a Trinity of Persons. In holy Love the Father eternally begets the Son and spirates the Holy Spirit: thus the Holy Trinity is a Trinity of Love. From the Father through the Son and by the Holy Spirit all Love flows both in creation and in redemption. As St John stated it: "God so loved the world that he gave His only begotten Son..." (John 3:16).

Finally, from Paul's writings I must mention the prayer-request of the apostle in Ephesians 3:14ff., where he kneels in prayer to the Father in heaven and longs that "Christ may dwell in your hearts by faith: that ye, being rooted and grounded in love, may be able to comprehend with all saints what is the breadth, and length, and depth, and height: and to know the love of Christ which passeth knowledge, that ye might be filled with all the fullness of God." I doubt if the theme of this book can be better expressed than Paul has done for us here. To know God is to be filled with the love of God but it is also at the same time to recognize and to understand that God who is Love is greater than our highest thoughts and beyond our loftiest contemplation of Him. For the God who is present as the Holy Spirit (or the Spirit of Christ) in His Church and covenant people is the God who is also utterly transcendent, beyond space and time, and glorious in His holiness and Majesty.

The Divine Love in Liturgy

The Common Prayer Tradition captures this great theme of the holy love of God in a variety of ways. God's love in creating and maintaining the world is affirmed as an expression of His goodness. There is a full and always moving presentation of the love of God manifested in Jesus Christ, in his mission, passion, death, resurrection and exaltation. Likewise the sending by the Father through the Son of the Holy Spirit is presented as a further manifestation of God's love as well as the provision of that love to be the holy content of the souls, hearts, minds and wills of those who believe on the name of the Lord Jesus.

So we may join James I Packer in explaining God's love in this way: "God's love is an exercise of His goodness towards individual sinners whereby, having identified Himself with their welfare, He has given His Son to be their Saviour, and now brings them to know and enjoy Him in a covenant relation" (*Knowing God*, 1973, p.111). From the beginning of this book I have sought to explain not only that we know God because He first chooses to know us but also that our knowing of each other is always within the covenant relation, which He establishes. How this works in the Common Prayer Tradition with respect to God as holy love and pure goodness we must now briefly survey.

Baptism and Confirmation exist as Sacraments because of the holy love of God. There is a Gospel to proclaim since God so loved the world that He gave His only-begotten Son to die for our sins and to be raised for our justification. Messengers are sent into the world by the Lord Jesus because in His love He has provided salvation for all who will believe upon His holy Name. "Go ye therefore, and teach all nations, baptizing them in the name of the Father and of the Son and of the Holy Ghost: teaching them to observe all things whatsoever I have commanded you" (Matt.28:19-20). Love calls sinners and in the love of God they believe and are baptized into His covenant to enjoy His steadfast, faithful love.

The Daily Office exists as the appointed means and way of being encountered by God because of His holy love and goodness. God mercifully calls His covenant people to be with Him, to recognize His Majesty, to confess their sins, to hear His Word, to receive His forgiveness and salvation, to petition Him and to intercede with Him and to know Him as LORD. In this daily discipline centred upon God's self-revelation recorded in Scripture and celebrated in Psalms and Canticles there is a growing awareness of the height and depth, the breadth and length of the holy love of God. The soul gradually lays aside all human conceptions of love and is drawn into the mind of Christ to share his love.

We may say that through reading and meditating upon Scripture in the Daily Office God's covenant people are truly taught the nature and meaning, as well as the practice of love. Their prayers, flowing from this formative reading, become more and more the prayers of love for the brethren and expressions of the love of God shed abroad in their hearts by the Holy Spirit. We may claim that the Litany is the fullest expression in Liturgy of love addressing the Lord of love in petition and intercession.

The Holy Communion is pre-eminently the Sacrament of the holy love of God. Here is the Love which forgives, cleanses, justifies, sanctifies, unites to Christ and feeds with heavenly manna at the heavenly table. This is the holy love so splendidly described in the Proper Prefaces for Christmas-Day, Easter-Day, Ascension-Day, Whit-Sunday and the Feast of the Holy Trinity. And it is the love which as goodness and mercy is recognized and celebrated in the Prayer of Consecration:

Almighty God, our heavenly Father, who of thy tender mercy didst give thine only Son, Jesus Christ, to suffer death upon the Cross for our redemption; who made there (by His one oblation of himself once offered) a full, perfect, and sufficient sacrifice, oblation and satisfaction for the sins of the whole world...

In the words "full, perfect and sufficient" we hear what love achieved and what we never could have earned and certainly do not deserve. Then, having been fed by God at the Holy Table of His Son we cannot but pray:

Almighty and ever living God, we most heartily thank thee, for that thou dost vouchsafe to feed us, who have duly received these holy mysteries, with the spiritual food of the most precious Body and Blood of thy Son our Saviour Jesus Christ; and dost assure us thereby of thy favour and goodness towards us; and that we are very members incorporate in the mystical body of thy Son...

Being fed on heavenly manna is only part of the revelation of the love of God. There is the inner assurance of the covenant favor and grace and tender mercy of God for believing sinners; and there is communion and union with the Lord Jesus Christ, wherein spirit speaks to Spirit. This is knowledge indeed!

In the Visitation of the Sick God's tender mercy, love and goodness are the divine realities which make this event meaningful and necessary. Love is expressed in the opening salutation: "Peace be to this house, and to all that dwell in it." It is then assumed in everything which follows. The purpose of the service is that the sick person may hear God's gracious promises and truly know God and be known by Him. Whether he is to recover or whether he is to die the aim is to make sure that he is in a right relationship with God and knows that God is Love and in Christ loves him now. Thus after Psalms and Collects the priest says:

The Almighty Lord, who is a strong tower to all those who put their trust in him, to whom all things in heaven,

*in earth, and under the earth, do bow and obey; be now
and evermore thy defence; and make thee know and feel,
that there is no other Name under heaven given to man,
in whom, and through whom. thou mayest receive health
and salvation, but only the Name of the Lord Jesus
Christ. Amen.*

In sickness and in pain it is truly good *to know and feel*
the promises and presence of the Lord Jesus Christ.

Finally, we note that the Burial of the Dead is based
wholly on the doctrine of the love of God in Jesus Christ
which pardons sin and gives the gift of eternal life to all who
receive the Gospel. The first words are the wonderful promise of Jesus Christ: "I am the resurrection and the life..."
God's comfort is communicated to those who mourn
through familiar Psalms and through the reading of 1 Corinthians 15, the classic New Testament passage on the resurrection of the dead and the glorious life with Christ in the
age to come. In an optional Collect the continuing knowing
of God both by the departed and the living is recognized until
the Second Coming of the Lord Jesus, the general resurrection of the dead and the blessed life of the age to come.

*O Almighty God, the God of the spirits of all flesh, who
by thy voice from heaven didst proclaim, Blessed are the
dead who die in the Lord; Multiply, we beseech thee, to
those who rest in Jesus, the manifold blessings of thy
love, that the good work which thou didst begin in them
may be perfected unto the day of Jesus Christ. And of
thy mercy, O heavenly Father, vouchsafe that we, who
now serve thee on earth, may at last, together with them,
be found meet partakers of the inheritance of the saints
in light; for the sake of the same thy Son, Jesus Christ
our Lord.*

Both the dead and the living await the resurrection of
the dead and what has been termed the beatific vision, the
beholding of the glory of God in the face of Jesus Christ,
Incarnate God.

Conclusion

Finally, with many others I always feel deeply moved when I join in the familiar but profound prayer called "A General Thanksgiving:"

Almighty God, Father of all mercies, we thine unworthy servants do give thee most humble and heart thanks for all thy goodness and loving-kindness to us, and to all men. We bless thee for our creation, preservation, and all the blessings of this life; but above all, for thine inestimable love in the redemption of the world by our Lord Jesus Christ; for the means of grace, and for the hope of glory. And, we beseech thee, give us that due sense of all thy mercies, that our hearts may be unfeignedly thankful; and that we show forth thy praise not only with our lips but in our lives, by giving up ourselves to thy service, and by walking before thee in holiness and righteousness all our days; through Jesus Christ our Lord, to whom, with thee and the Holy Ghost, be all honour and glory, world without end. Amen.

Where this prayer is truly the prayer of the mind-in-the-heart of God's covenant people, it may be said of them that they know the Lord. May we all join with St Paul in concluding: "I count all things but loss for the excellency of the knowledge of Christ Jesus, my Lord" (Phil.3:8). Thanks be to God the Father whom we know in the Son and by the Holy Spirit both in Liturgy and in our daily vocations. *Amen.*